GOD GOES TO HIGH SCHOOL

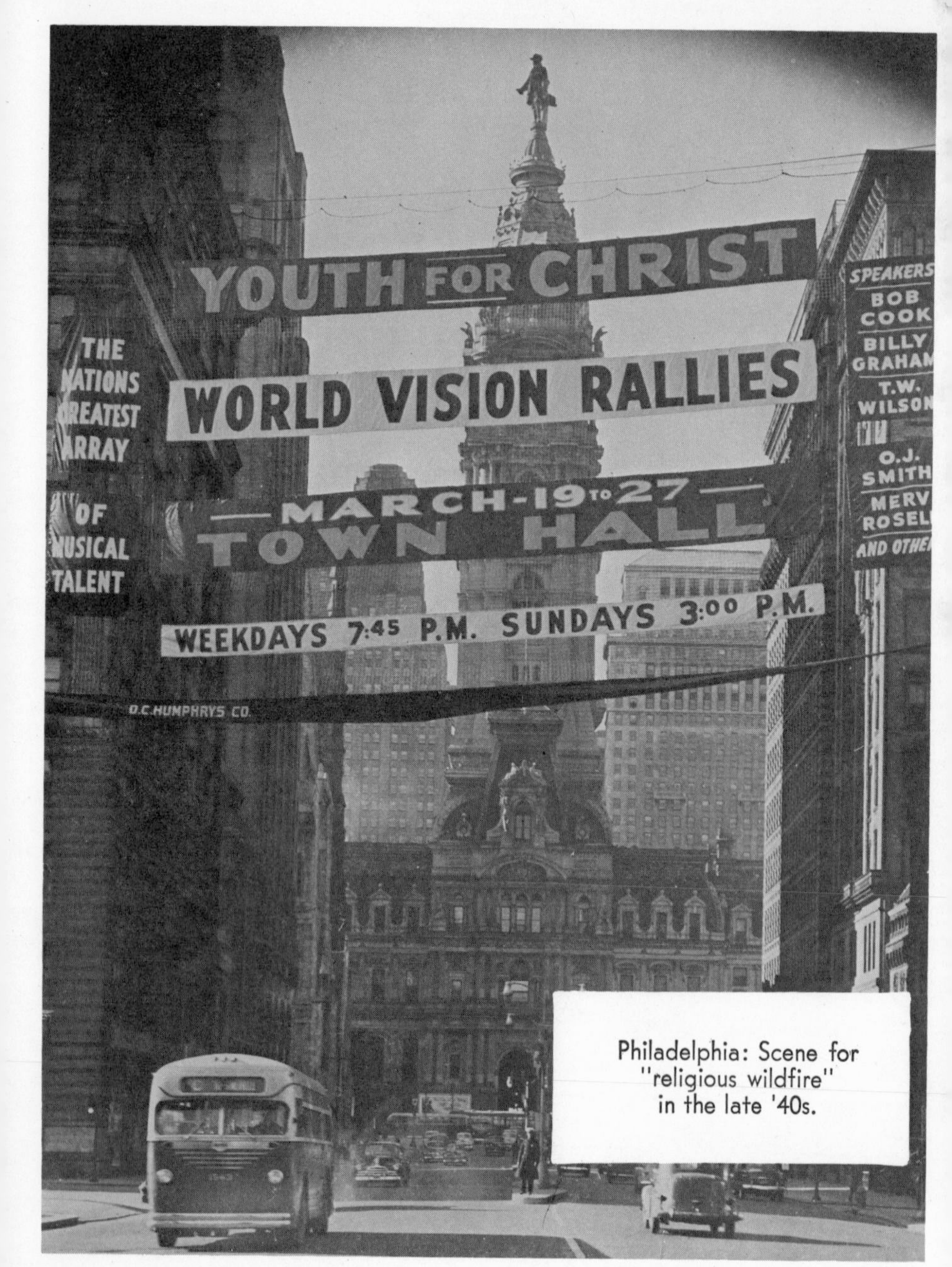

Philadelphia: Scene for "religious wildfire" in the late '40s.

For your church library -
Thank you for your
faithfulness ~
Phil. 1:6

Don & Peg Windmiller

GOD GOES TO HIGH SCHOOL

JAMES HEFLEY

WORD BOOKS, Publisher

Waco, Texas *London, England*

GOD GOES TO HIGH SCHOOL

First Printing—September 1970
Second Printing—May 1971

4800 W. Waco Drive
Waco, Texas 76710

Printed in the United States of America.
Library of Congress catalog card number: 75-85830

CONTENTS

Preface 7

PART I. YOUTH FOR CHRIST—THE GROWING YEARS

Chapter
1 "A-hootin' and A-hollerin' for Jesus . . ." 13
2 The Torch Lighters 28
3 Something on the Counters 42
4 The Spin-Offs 58
5 Guiding the Race Horses 70
6 Voyage into a New Era 83

PART II. YOUTH FOR CHRIST TODAY

7 Shock It to Me 99
8 Tale of Five Cities 119
9 The New Evangelists 137
10 YFC Around the World 153
11 YFC—A Continuing Miracle? 172

Postscript: A Look at YFC Personnel 184

Appendix 189

PREFACE

All books have a beginning and this one started one fine summer afternoon when Floyd Thatcher of Word Books dropped by with a representative of Youth for Christ. They wanted me to write a book about YFC because, as they said, "You know nothing about the subject."

My pride took a nosedive, and I looked at them blankly.

"You are *not* acquainted with Youth for Christ, are you?" Floyd asked.

I shrugged. "Not really. I've seen their magazine and have written some articles for it. When in New Orleans, I spoke two or three times for some meetings called Youth for Christ. That's about all."

"That's what we want," the YFC man explained. "With our cooperation we want you to look us over and write what you see."

I had heard that before. Few organizations really want an objective book written about them—a book that shines a light into every dark and wished-to-be-forgotten corner of the past. When I was convinced that they really meant it, I accepted the assignment.

I began my research as a curious outsider, one who realized that most teens will never be won to Christ within church buildings, one whose oldest daughter, Cynthia, became a teen last year.

Throughout, YFC permitted me to maintain an independent stance. All financial arrangements were between the publisher and me. I pored over 15,000 pages of old YFC magazines, minutes, and other records; talked to scores of former and present YFC personnel; sat in on rallies, club meetings, board meetings, training seminars, and teen bull sessions around the world. I found alumni in strange places—for example, the headwaters of the Amazon (a Wycliffe Bible translator) and Houston's Manned Spacecraft Center (an Apollo astronaut).

I was impressed, inspired, amused, and disgusted. Most impressive was the refreshing openness of YFC personnel and their willingness to admit mistakes. "We goofed on that one" or "We didn't act like Christians in that situation" were some of the honest expressions of failure I heard.

I can't recall anyone within the present YFC organization dodging a question. I did get the feeling that two or three old-timers were trying to brush me off with generalities during interviews.

After months of research, I realized that on one hand the book could be slanted as a devastating evangelical exposé or—the other extreme—it could be palmed off as a glorious puff. I have tried to follow neither extreme. I have simply attempted to tell what I've seen, heard, and read about Youth for Christ's present and past and let the reader form his own opinions.

Astute readers close to certain events and people may see mistakes and incorrect judgments. For such I take full responsibility and plead only naïve sincerity as an outsider.

One should not give away the story in the preface, but I will say that parents and church leaders who are concerned about youth should know what YFC has done and is doing now. If history repeats itself, the various churches will be doing in 1975 what YFC is doing today. This simply reflects the truism that capable independent specialists in any field, whether nuclear physics or youth evangelism, will be ahead of the generalists, who, fortunately, can profit from the mistakes and successes of the pioneers.

Finally, I thank those who made it possible for me to do this book: Word Books through its senior editor, Floyd Thatcher, and his capable staff; YFC through its personnel, who granted untold hours of interviews; former YFC personnel who did the same; and YFC teens in the United States and several countries abroad. I especially thank Harold Myra, editor of *Campus Life*, and Ron Wilson, Youth for Christ Overseas Literature director, for journalistic assistance. Ron, in particular, provided anecdotes from his long experience with teens.

Closer to home, I thank Mrs. Paula Kelly for her usual good secretarial work, and my wife, Marti, for assisting with the research, editing final copy, and offering frank criticism. Marti also grew up apart from Youth for Christ. Her frequent comment in editing the book was, "Wow, would I like to have been in on that when I was a teen!"

JAMES HEFLEY

Arlington Heights, Illinois

PART I

YOUTH FOR CHRIST— THE GROWING YEARS

1

"A-hootin' and A-hollerin' for Jesus . . ."

What was it?

Harry Golden, the Jewish sage from Charlotte, called it "an entirely different brand of 'nativism,' " with "thousands of boys and girls a-hootin' and a-hollerin' for Jesus to the beat of a drum and to the orders of a few spielers."

A European theologian decried it as "wild gyrations" that try to evangelize with a "fundamentalist circus horse" that paws the ground three times in answering the question: "How many persons are there in the Trinity?"

Ma Sunday exulted, "I haven't seen anything like this since the days of my husband, Billy."

General Douglas MacArthur invited it to Japan to "provide the surest foundation for the firm establishment of democracy in the land where the emperor has ceased to be a god."

Torrey Johnson, the first president, cited Youth for Christ as "God's proof that it's possible to get large crowds out to hear God's Word on The Devil's Night."

Newspaper magnate William Randolph Hearst saw it as a "good and growing thing" that "will never be good enough or big enough until it involves all of our young people in this country." He ordered his editors to produce headline copy, and there was no lack of it in those days. The country was locked in a furor of patriotic passion. Americans lined up for ration coupons, turned in every spare ounce of fat for munitions, and anxiously charted Allied progress across Europe toward the heart of the Third Reich.

Whatever else Youth for Christ was in those waning months of World War II, it was religious wildfire. And, thanks to Hearst and other publicity puffers, YFC bannered the front pages from Kalispell to Kokomo, fanning the flames, as hundreds of "rallies" sprang up to spread the fire.

Every rally followed a pattern: Saturday night in a big church or auditorium. Interdenominational. Enthusiasm. A youth orchestra and choir with quartets, trios, and soloists. Bible quizzes. "Popcorn" testimonies punctuated with, "Praise the Lord." An emcee with a roving microphone for on-the-spot surprise introductions. Witty and earnest "name" preachers, athletes, military heroes, and business and civic leaders as speakers. A call to "walk the aisle" for salvation, dedication, or surrender to full-time service. Decision makers were referred to a "Bible-preaching, Christ-honoring church" of their choice.

The song leader cleaved the air, keeping time to up-tempo songs while alternately singing and shouting, "Sing it! Sing it!" The preacher paced the stage like a nervous squirrel in a cage, microphone cord trailing behind like an umbilical cord, waving his arms, and shouting anathemas against sin (smoking, dancing, movie attendance, petting, and other forms of worldliness) and modernism. Sometimes he'd take a dig at institutional church life, but always proclaiming Christ's sacrifice as the only means of salvation.

Floyd Ankerberg in Kansas City actually wrenched his arm out of joint while stressing a sermon point. He called for a doctor to meet him off the platform. With the dislocated limb reset, Ankerberg returned and completed his sermon.

The program personalities sported broad, brashy, wide ties or bright-colored bow ties, some of which blinked from battery-powered lights when the crowd chorused "This Little Light of Mine." When glo-sox caught on in the teen world, the YFC men stocked up on the gaudiest colors they could find, then traded around before going on stage so the audience would have fun guessing who's wearing what in the leg show. Sober-faced young divinity students who spouted the neo-orthodoxy of theologians Barth and Brunner dubbed the YFC rally directors "fundies," or "neon-orthodoxies."

The neon-orthodoxies vied to see who could serve God with

Above: The "old-time" demonstrators bring them in for a rally in Memphis. **Below:** YFC was big in Cleveland. The local rally entered this float in the St. Patrick's Day parade.

YFC was "evangelical vaudeville" at its best. Here Chief White Feather sings for Vancouver, British Columbia, YFC.

At an early rally ten thousand jammed into Minneapolis Municipal Auditorium . . . and thousands more were turned away.

the most unusual talent. God's inventive geniuses found it hard to top Willis Shank, Seattle's YFC director and "Most Outstanding Young Man in 1947." Shank could make a battered oil can with one string sound like a cello solo in a symphony. He also "played" musical glasses, a saxophone, a saw, a violin, and whistled.

But the attraction that got the most attention (and the most criticism from shocked churchmen) was "MacArthur the Gospel Horse." He knelt before an improvised cross while the choir sang, "Kneel at the Cross." He moved his jaws to show "how the girls in the choir chew gum" and displayed Bible knowledge by responding to quiz questions. For "How many apostles?" he gave twelve hoof taps. For "How many Persons in the Trinity?" he gave three taps. This answer often brought a comment from the emcee that "MacArthur knows more than the modernists." A correct answer was rewarded with an orange; a miss got him a grapefruit. Billy Graham complained that the horse got the biggest advertising headline when he and the animal were booked for the same rally. Dr. M. R. DeHaan once came to the podium while the rally director was shovelling up an "accident." The gravel-voiced radio evangelist growled, "This horse may be a Christian, but he's no gentleman."

For "separated" fundamentalist kids who didn't moon and swoon over Sinatra or jitterbug to a juke box, YFC was the place to go on Saturday night. For homesick soldiers stationed in a strange town, YFC was better than walking the streets or hanging around the canteen. For curiosity seekers (many of whom were converted) it was a free show. For adults tired of dreary church rituals and sermons in monotones, YFC furnished excitement and a nostalgic return to youth.

With fast-moving programs that combined Christian vaudeville and fervent revival-style preaching, YFC packed in hundreds of thousands throughout the United States and Canada while crusty religious leaders gaped in surprise. "What do you think of YFC?" was the burning question in seminary classrooms from Princeton to Berkeley. While many seminary students, professors, and clergy gaped, gawked, and snickered under their Barthian breaths, YFC marched on.

Bright young graduates of Wheaton College, Bob Jones University, Taylor University, Moody Bible Institute, Nyack Missionary College, and other theologically conservative schools preached and pounded the old-time religion to Saturday night thousands. They stood under banners proclaiming "Old-Fashioned Truth for Up-to-date Youth," "A Traction for a Slipping World," and the slogan which became the motto for YFC, "Geared to the Times, but Anchored to the Rock."

And they came, mostly the young but many not so young: 75,000 in Chicago; 18,000 in Detroit; 20,000 in Los Angeles; 6,500 in Winnipeg; 12,000 in Minneapolis. And when they left, thousands had come to the front of an auditorium, chapel, stadium, or hall to give their lives to God at the invitation of an evangelist. For, again, whatever else it might have been, it was the means which brought untold thousands of young men and women to a new life in Jesus Christ.

Even while the critics were predicting, "It won't last," the fire leaped the oceans. Puffed and programmed by missionaries and Christian GIs, YFC American-style rallies sprang up in over a hundred foreign cities from Peking to Brussels.

The flames flickered and died in many places during the forties, but more fires broke out elsewhere in the fifties. Slowly the movement solidified into an organization, spread onto the high-school campuses with weekday Bible clubs, dropped some old methods and adopted some new ones. It snuggled closer to the church, and finally became the international organization that is evangelizing teens in fifty-four countries today.

Where, when, and by whom did it all begin? The answer to this three-pronged question is elusive—perhaps it is best to say that the origin and originators of YFC can never be packed into a single unassailable statement.

Journalist Robert Raikes started the first vital youth ministry of modern times when in 1781 he hired four women to teach reading and writing to street youth on weekdays and the Bible on Sunday. From Raikes' classes came the Sunday school which church leaders first condemned, then copied.

Exactly a century after Raikes started the first Sunday school, Maine pastor Francis E. Clark organized the Christian Endeavor Society to harness the youth of his church for service. The movement soon became interdenominational and world-wide.

Two years later Scottish army officer William Smith, a convert under Moody, organized the first "Boys' Brigade" to promote discipline and Bible study among street boys.

Inter-Varsity Christian Fellowship, the Young Men's Christian Association, the Young Women's Christian Association, and the Student Volunteer Movement followed during the latter half of the nineteenth century. But their thrust was mainly to college and young working people, not to high schoolers.

The twentieth century gave birth to the National Young Life Campaign (1911) under two English preacher brothers who felt they should specialize in winning youth. Frederick Wood, one of the brothers, came to America for meetings under the Christian Youth Campaign of America headed by fiery Lloyd Bryant. On their tour they met seminary student Jim Rayburn, and assisted financially by Methodist businessman Herbert Taylor of Chicago, Rayburn began Young Life in 1937, the organization which today most closely resembles Youth for Christ.

Lloyd Bryant was the first "youth rally director" in America. His concern for millions of American youth with no religious affiliation moved him to start a youth broadcast in 1929 and direct thrice-weekly rallies for seven years in Manhattan in the Christian and Missionary Alliance Tabernacle. And in 1935 he toured America with the film *Youth Marches On,* sparking interest for youth rallies in numerous cities.

A year later Christian Youth Fellowship meetings were started in Washington, and within six months youth from twenty-one denominations and fifty-six congregations were attending. Percy Crawford launched his Young People's Church of the Air in 1931. His rapid-fire, Scripture-punctuated sermons became models for future YFC evangelists.

Across the border in Brantford, Ontario, a young Australian, Paul Guiness, started, in 1934, the first interdenominational youth rally in North America under the name "Youth for Christ." * Brantford YFC met in a rented theater, brought in outside speakers, and attracted crowds up to five hundred. Several other Canadian cities picked up the idea, but not always

*This same year an interdenominational Christian youth movement in Russia had as its motto "Youth for Christ."

the name, and began holding interdenominational youth rallies.

The same year Brantford YFC began, Walter Smyth in Philadelphia initiated a youth center with fourteen people that grew and became part of the mushrooming movement.

Oscar Gillian started a broadcast and rally in southern California called Voice of Christian Youth. He sent out gospel teams to evangelize in interdenominational youth rallies.

Gillian moved to Detroit in 1937 where he jointly pastored a Presbyterian Church and initiated an interdenominational VCY rally under the motto "Youth for Christ." But he soon became restless again and moved to Vancouver where he started another VCY. Detroit VCY continued under Ed Darling.

At the urging of Percy Crawford, a converted dance band trombonist named Jack Wyrtzen launched a youth broadcast in 1940. As interest mounted, he moved his "Word of Life" broadcast from a small station to powerful 50,000-watt WHN in Manhattan. He also held rallies to back the broadcast in the Christian and Missionary Alliance Tabernacle near Times Square where Lloyd Bryant had preached a few years before.

Wyrtzen patterned his style after Percy Crawford. As his broadcast expanded to more stations, he inspired other young evangelists to start broadcasts with the same format—peppy uptempo music and punchy youth testimonies, climaxed by a rousing evangelistic sermon.

Thus Bryant, Gillian, Guiness, Crawford, and Wyrtzen became the principal seed-planters and pace-setters for this giant of all youth movements soon to emerge. Notably, few reached into the South. There the majority Southern Baptists had moved ahead of other denominations with their Sunday evening Baptist Young People's Union that sponsored interchurch rallies for Baptist youth.

Suddenly—Pearl Harbor . . . and the United States was plunged into the world conflict that had been raging in Europe for over two years. The Japanese rolled over the Philippines, Malaya, Burma, Indonesia, and many Pacific islands, destroyed an Allied fleet and by mid-1942 reached the Aleutian Islands—while Hitler's juggernaut had driven to the English channel and deep into Russia and North Africa.

A flood of patriotism swept the United States and Canada as

able-bodied men marched to war and women manned the defense plants. War taxes skyrocketed. Gasoline rationing kept people close to their homes and radios. Jack Wyrtzen, with his God-bless-America and hurrah-for-Jesus youth programs, brightened the airways and attracted bigger crowds to see the broadcast live.

Roger Malsbary, a Christian and Missionary Alliance evangelist, picked up the cue from Wyrtzen and started a combination broadcast-rally in the old English Theater in Indianapolis May 29, 1943. Malsbary called his rally "Youth for Christ," the first to bear the name YFC in the United States. ("I asked myself, 'What are you trying to do? Reach *youth for Christ!*' ")

Malsbary's success inspired his fellow C&MA preacher Dick Harvey in St. Louis to start a YFC rally the first Saturday night in February, 1944, with the silver-tongued Southern Baptist pastor Dr. Robert G. Lee from Memphis as speaker.* Across the state in Kansas City, a young 4-F preacher named Al Metsker had already started "Christian Youth of Kansas City."

Back in New York, Wyrtzen moved into Carnegie Hall. Then for a special April Fool's Day rally in 1944, he rented Madison Square Garden. Twenty thousand jammed inside and another ten thousand were turned away. The radio-announced attendance astounded and challenged youth-minded preachers throughout the U.S. and Canada. More began dreaming of what might be done in other cities.

Wyrtzen in New York, Malsbary in Indianapolis, Harvey in St. Louis, and Metsker in Kansas City made George Wilson in Minneapolis feel something big was on tap in the singspiration planned as the feature of the annual Homecoming Week at Northwestern Bible School. His well-advertised meeting in Minneapolis, April 29, 1944, drew three thousand youth into the First Baptist Church. When he asked, "Would you like another singspiration in two weeks?" they roared back, "Yes!"

A dark-haired young Chicago pastor who turned up to observe Wilson's next "singspiration" was late and had to stand. Torrey Johnson had already seen Indianapolis and St. Louis and he

*Malsbary's first guest speaker was also a Baptist, Dr. Henry H. Savage from Michigan.

knew about Jack Wyrtzen. The young radio singer Beverly Shea and other Chicagoans had been begging him to "start something for the soldiers." And after a midnight prayer meeting at the National Association of Evangelicals convention in Columbus, Ohio, he told his secretary Amy Anderson, "We're going to have a youth rally in Chicago. I don't know who or where or what with, but I know we're going to reach these young servicemen who are walking the streets."

What Torrey Johnson saw in Minneapolis gave him more assurance that "God was going to do something in Chicago." He quickly hired his young brother-in-law, Bob Cook, as associate pastor of the new Midwest Bible Church that already had the second largest Sunday evening congregation in Chicago. Bob could play trombone, lead singing and handle publicity—valuable talents for a youth rally. Torrey also tapped Billy Graham, then pastor of the Village Church in nearby Western Springs and preacher for the popular "Songs in the Night" radio broadcast, which Torrey had founded, to be the preacher. He found a meeting place at prestigious Orchestra Hall and booked a half-hour on Radio WCFL.

When Amy wondered, "Where will you get the money?" Torrey replied impatiently, "The Lord's got the money."

Several times as the date for the first rally approached Amy heard Torrey, Billy and Bob praying, "Lord, put this meeting on a miracle basis." More than once Billy stopped in her office and paced the floor while saying nervously, "You gotta pray for me. You gotta pray a lot."

Saturday night, May 27, 1944, came—ten days before D-day and one year after the first YFC rally in Indianapolis. In a downstairs room in Orchestra Hall emcee Torrey, song leader Bob Cook, preacher Billy Graham, organist Doug Fisher, soloist Rose Arzoomanian, Amy, and several others prayed. "Lord, put this meeting on a miracle basis."

They walked into the auditorium and stood in awe. Even the gallery was packed. And the crowds kept coming to Orchestra Hall all summer long.

Chicago was even then the off-center center of the U.S. It led the nation in the war effort—in production of war goods, sale of bonds, enlistments, and salvage collection. It was the economic, agricultural, industrial, and cultural heart of America, and with its big crowds and powerful publicity, the Chicago rally quickly became the focal point of the North American Saturday night youth rallies. Letters poured in from distant cities begging advice on how to start their own. Amy and other women from the Midwest Bible Church frequently worked far into the night, writing letters and stuffing envelopes.

The Chicago success started an epidemic. Like chicken pox in an elementary school, rallies began popping up all over the globe. Challenged by letters from home, Christian GIs held rallies as they advanced with the Allied forces in the Pacific and in Europe. Often the first thing they did after occupying a town was to hang out a banner on a main street announcing where the Youth for Christ rally would meet the next Saturday night.

Doubtless the Orchestra Hall crowds and those around the country were evidence of war-spurred religious interest. Things had changed from the apathetic thirties, and when promoters waved the flag as well as the Bible—the formula for many early YFC rallies—they filled the auditorium.

It happened in New York, Chicago, Minneapolis, Indianapolis, St. Louis, and Kansas City. They came by the thousands in Toronto, Winnipeg, Boston, Montreal, Havana, Paris and elsewhere.

On October 21, 1944, Chicagoland YFC (which Torrey directed without salary), packed in thirty thousand for a Victory Rally at Chicago Stadium. Torrey emceed, world champion indoor miler Gil Dodds testified, Bev Shea and Rose Arzoomanian sang, and Merv Rosell preached. An Andy Frain usher observed the crowd, remembered presidential candidate Tom Dewey's appearance in the stadium, and cracked, "Whataya know! More people got religion in Chicago than belong to the Republican Party!"

With the flames burning around the world, an international organization had to come, not to smother the flames but to channel them in orderly and fruitful directions, to hold down the excesses, and keep out the con men.

Roger Malsbary first suggested the idea of an organizing convention. Arthur W. McKee, executive director of the Winona Lake (Indiana) Bible Conference, pledged to host all who could attend. In August, 1944, eight men met at Winona for a lengthy prayer meeting and a conference. Roger Malsbary, Torrey Johnson, Bob Cook, Dick Harvey from St. Louis, Ed Darling from Detroit, Ray Schulenberg from Moline, Illinois, Palmer Muntz (the Bible Conference's program director), and Arthur W. McKee agreed to pray every day until they met again in November. Neither Jack Wyrtzen nor Percy Crawford were on hand. Both were busy in their own bailiwicks, and Wyrtzen, belonging to the unorganized Brethren fellowship, did not want to join in any binding associations.

In November a larger group of thirty-five men from twenty-one cities convened in Detroit and elected Torrey Johnson chairman of a "Temporary Youth for Christ International Committee" that included Wheaton College President V. Raymond Edman, Harvey, Malsbary, and Schulenberg.

Between then and the next summer the requests for help became a deluge. The "Temporary Committee" set up a "temporary" YFCI * office in Chicago to handle the inquiries and service existing rallies wanting assistance. Torrey had to have help.

Billy Graham was in Florida, recuperating from a severe case of the mumps that had kept him from becoming an Army chaplain. Torrey went looking for him in Miami, took him fishing, and while out in the boat spelled out his dream for YFCI's future. He proposed that Billy become the first full-time organizer and evangelist for YFCI. Billy agreed, but only with the stipulation of "not one bit of paper work." Back in Chicago, Torrey hired a Christian printer, Clyde Dennis, to edit the YFC magazine taken over from Indianapolis.

When Billy returned, recovered from the mumps, Torrey told his secretary, "Get on the phone and start booking him in rallies and churches."

Amy Anderson started calling and got mostly negative responses. Over and over she heard, "Billy Graham? We've never heard of him. We don't want an unknown quantity."

When she apprised Torrey of the problem, he snorted, "Keep at it. The world is going to hear from this young man."

*YFCI from this point on refers to Youth for Christ International.

For Memorial Day, 1945, Torrey planned the "biggest youth rally yet." It had been an eventful spring and the country was high on a wave of emotion. Roosevelt had died in April. Several weeks later Russian and American troops embraced on the Elbe, and two weeks after that the Germans surrendered. In less than a month the *Queen Mary* would dock in New York harbor carrying the first load of returning veterans.

So Torrey rented mammoth Soldiers Field. When advance pledges didn't meet the need, he mortgaged his home. When weather forecasters predicted rain, he prayed, "Lord, put this meeting on a miracle basis." A torrent of rain fell the evening before Memorial Day; at rally time 75,000 sat under a star-studded sky.

Chicago had never seen anything like it. Five hundred uniformed nurses marched past a large lighthouse erected for the occasion and formed a living white cross before the platform. The war dead were honored in a solemn ceremony; then a 5,000-voice (white-robed) choir sang, accompanied by a 300-member band and eight grand pianos. Gil Dodds ran two spotlighted laps and gave a testimony. Navy chaplain and war hero Bob Evans, resplendent in uniform, gave his testimony. Representatives of China, India, Africa, and Russia in native dress joined in a missionary pageant. Percy Crawford preached and appealed for those "moved by the Holy Spirit" to hand decision cards to the ushers. Hundreds did. The choir sang "Shine on Me" while a circular spotlight revolved upon the great crowd.

It was a night when Billy Graham, Torrey Johnson, Bob Cook (who directed the rally), and other young preachers saw more than stars in the clear sky. So did the Hearst newspapers. One month later every one of the twenty-two papers in the chain carried a full-page story and pictures on the national movement that was reaching half a million youth each Saturday night.

On July 22, 1945, the forty-two delegates met for the founding YFCI convention in Winona Lake. Hearst's Wesley Hartzell, himself a delegate, was there and wrote:

"Much of the same atmosphere of enthusiasm and energy must have characterized the early church fathers who streamed in from every section of the then-known world to attend the

Nicean Council. But these young men are not gathered to outline a new creed or religion. They are here to bring new methods into the Christian faith, to draw young people back to the church and found their every deed upon the Bible."

Torrey Johnson keynoted the conference. In many ways this confident and imaginative young pastor embodied religious wildfire. He believed God could do anything and wouldn't listen when men said no. He was a general who was at his best in the conference room, communicating his own vision and convincing the skeptics.

When he spoke that summer day he was aware that America was one—pulling together in a big nationwide effort as it never had before. So he told the delegates that "the youth movement has grown and spread so rapidly that it is no longer possible for cities to isolate themselves from one another, but we must 'sink or swim together.' . . . The eyes of the whole country are on us. . . . Fundamentalism is looking to YFC with hope; modernism with apprehension; the vast majority of people are . . . in between. Right now we are carrying the ball."

Then the forty-two * declared themselves official delegates to the first convention and set about the business of electing a president. The nominating committee presented only two names: Dick Harvey and Torrey Johnson. Harvey decided to withdraw and Torrey was elected unanimously.

Then Torrey declined to accept. But they begged him to reconsider and not make a final refusal until after private prayer.

Wednesday after midnight, Torrey prayed alone on the lakeshore. The next morning he made his formal acceptance.

The constitution they voted included the doctrinal platform held by the one-year-old National Association of Evangelicals.

*The forty-two: V. R. Edman, Maurice Carlson, Brig. Richard Fitton (Salvation Army), John Huffman, Torrey Johnson, Hubert Mitchell, Carroll Shuster, Charles Templeton, Clay Cooper, John Dunlap, William Erny, Everett Graffam, Bob Jones, Jr., Bob Pierce, Hyman Appleman, Thomas Field, Roger Malsbary, Jess Moody, Walter Smyth, George Wilson, Archer Weniger, Douglas Fisher, Dick Harvey, Julius Johnson, Clare Richardson, Ellis Howe, Ray Schulenberg, Elmer Standley, Ed Darling, John Brown, Rheinhold Barth, Bob Cook, Louis Paul Lehman, Frank Phillips, Mitchell Seidler, Bob Finley, Billy Graham, Emerson Pent, Wesley Hartzell, J. Elwin Wright, Arthur McKee and J. Palmer Muntz.

The NAE statement of faith proclaimed the "essentials" of evangelical Christianity upon which about fifty small denominations could unite (acceptance of the deity of Christ; the Bible as God's "inspired, infallible" Word; and other specifics). It was their answer to the liberal, "modernistic" denial of historic doctrines within the ecumenically minded Protestant denominations.

So with a full slate of officers and a constitution, the first YFCI convention ended.* Only a few delegates had stayed to hear President Torrey (who had vowed to "cut loose and go out one hundred percent for YFCI") deliver an unofficial "inaugural" challenge in the Billy Sunday Tabernacle on Sunday morning.

"We shall not be satisfied with anything else or anything less than the complete evangelization of the world," he thundered. "God is in this thing and I hope you are."

Torrey Johnson delivers unofficial inaugural address to first YFCI convention.

*Dick Harvey was elected vice-president; George Wilson, secretary; and Walter Block from Kenosha, Wisconsin, treasurer.

The U.S. and Canada were divided into ten regions and ten men from the various regions elected regional vice-presidents: Bob Pierce, Pacific Northwest; Hubert Mitchell, Pacific Southwest; Rex Lindquist, Rocky Mountain; George Wilson, North Central; Dick Harvey, Central; Dan Iverson, South; John Huffman, New England; Ed Darling, Great Lakes; Walter Smyth, Eastern; Charles Templeton, Eastern Canada; Watson Argue, Western Canada.

None of the first four major officers and only one of the first ten regional veeps are officially related to YFC today. Bob Pierce is an at-large board member of North American YFCI.

2

The Torch Lighters

The war was over by fall of 1945. A happy spirit of thanksgiving filled the air. The boys began coming home even before the Japanese surrendered, and by the end of the year more than five million had been discharged. They returned to a world which, on the surface at least, seemed the same. But before the country lay some hard questions. Would there be a new army, this time of unemployed workers? As the country shifted to a peacetime economy, how much part should and could the government play? And leading the inquiring nation was an untested but thoroughly determined little man—Harry S. Truman.

While Truman struggled with economic conversion problems, Torrey moved YFC into high gear. He hired a business manager and executive secretary to run the YFC office. Ex-newspaper cartoonist Chuck Templeton prepared gimmicky publicity materials that a cadre of secretaries duplicated and sent out. The various rally directors mailed in attendance and decision reports and feature news for the YFC magazine.

The bigger rallies sometimes hired professional publicity men to puff big events, with the feeling that "if the devil's crowd can advertise and promote, so can we." But in Minneapolis a hired P.R. man called local reporters together before a news conference and whispered confidently, "If you want my opinion, this whole business is just a flash in a pan."

Many skeptical ministers thought so. They speculated that the crowds were seeking release from the repression of war and once having been through the emotional laundromat would return to dignity and more reasonable theology. Some were more catty. At the monthly pastors' conference, they picked apart the local YFC director, chuckled over his latest "extremes," and grumbled about "the kids in my church who are going crazy over these religious entertainers." Some were more charitable. One young denominational man remarked, "Well, at least it's better than crime."

Not all the critical clergymen were theological liberals. Fundamentalists who saw compromise in anything new complained that the "emotional rallies" were making a "mockery" of true worship. However, A. W. Tozer, respected conservative editor of the *Alliance Witness,* compared the critical fundamentalists to "army worms, who have for decades been following each other around the rim of their own little jars, each one afraid to step aside or hunt any new direction for himself, each slavishly following the other."

Confounding the skeptics and critics, YFCI rolled on. Rallies multiplied. Crowds grew. A second Memorial Day rally in Chicago's Soldiers Field brought out 75,000. This time the rains came but the speaker, Dr. Charles E. Fuller, stood up and asked calmly, "Please close your umbrellas. We're going to ask God to stop the rain." He prayed and the rain stopped.

Overseas, Americans enjoyed a liberator's popularity which they'd never known before (nor have since). They were from the wealthiest and strongest nation in the world, and Christian GIs had much going for them when they began YFC rallies in dozens of cities. Chaplains, GIs, missionaries, and a few Christian nationals got in the act. Torrey declared, "Who knows but what we've got an army of occupation for the purpose of establishing Youth for Christ."

In Paris under GI promotion and preaching, YFC started with thirty-five in a parish room of the American Cathedral and grew to pack out the American Methodist Church. In Manila a WAC trio sang and chaplains preached in a rented funeral parlor where the overflow crowd sat on coffin crates. GIs in Frankfurt rallied in the "Roundup Chapel," and published their own Frankfurt *Youth for Christ* magazine. A "United Nations" (before the world UN was established) gospel team of soldiers started a YFC rally in Westminster Chapel around the corner from London's Buckingham Palace and drew an audience of two thousand. Similar events took place in Okinawa, Guam, Seoul, Lisbon, Stockholm, Belfast, Oslo, Brussels, and Johannesburg.

Rally directors in North America and abroad could not keep their desks clean. As soon as one stack of decision cards had been funneled to churches, a new stack took its place. A hundred decisions in one night was not unusual. A name speaker like Torrey Johnson, Jack Shuler, or Merv Rosell might reap a thousand. Most rally directors sent decision cards straight to local churches. Many held follow-up classes with materials furnished by Dawson Trotman of The Navigators.

Dramatic conversion stories brightened the pages of the monthly YFCI magazine. In Oshkosh a boy known as "Little Dillinger" was converted from delinquency and called to the ministry. In Salt Lake City a girl on her way to the rally was stopped by a boy with a gun. She persuaded him to come along to the rally where he turned in his gun and was converted. In Chicago an estranged wife who had been picking up servicemen for companionship was converted in Orchestra Hall, and on the same Saturday night her sailor husband found a new life in the Los Angeles rally. After an exchange of letters they were reconciled.

Hundreds of young converts sped off to Christian training schools to train for the ministry and missionary service. For example, 111 students were found attending Canada's Prairie Bible Institute because of YFC. Even the exclusivist Southern Baptist Convention benefited from Baptist GIs who in YFC rallies overseas felt a "call" to service and came home to prepare.

Publishing executive Frank Mead, a strong denominational man, told off the critics in a strongly worded article in the venerable *Christian Herald*:

"We've offered youth everything from the Golden Gate Bridge to a 15¢ box of candy at Christmas . . . and still they leave us. We're giving them milk bars, gymnasiums, summer camps, rumpus rooms, and picnics—and they want none of it and none of us. We've made it ridiculously easy to join the church . . . we've made a lot of our churches 90% country club and 10% Gospel Hall—and along come . . . the Youth for Christ leaders, offering nothing but the unvarnished Gospel we thought they didn't want, asking them only that they change their whole way of thinking and their whole way of living. And youth goes for it, not in dribbles, not by twos and threes, but by thousands. Something goes on here that cannot be laughed off. What all the denominations have not been able to do, with all their resources, organization and highly trained experts, these men have done outside the church.

"Maybe they're wrong. . . . Only time and the Lord will tell us that. . . . But this much is as plain as the noses on our faces: This is a major religious phenomenon of our day stirring youth as youth has not been stirred for a generation.

"Is it they who are wrong, or we? Can it be that we have the wrong technique with youth in our churches?"

Something indeed was "going on." Torrey and his staff of YFCI field men were swamped with requests from rally directors, laymen, and pastors wanting to "reach the youth of our city."

Torrey had a direct way of saying to one or more of the six field men, "I believe God wants you to go" to Toronto, to Seattle, to Boston or to some other place where a speaker, an organizer, or a trouble-shooter was wanted. "Get the tickets, Amy." And off they flew at all hours and in all kinds of weather. It was Torrey's philosophy that "everyone can do something and it's my job to find out what it is and get him to do it."

Torrey's mood, and that of YFC, matched the national mood. Americans in late 1946 had begun a buying spree. Price controls were off. Truman had managed the impossible reconversion without the dreaded unemployment, but now both prices and wages soared. Business was bigger still and production was the key word.

Torrey's conviction that "God is in this thing" rubbed off on his field men. Once, for example, when Torrey couldn't make an engagement in Los Angeles, he wired for field evangelist Cliff Barrows to take his place. "Wheelbarrows" (as the combination song leader and preacher was known to many YFC men) wired back to Torrey, "Call nation to prayer. I can't make Los Angeles rally."

They were hot for God and the assurance that the hand of God was upon them kept the six field men moving, living out of duffel bags, losing weight, running hoarse from speaking three times a day, praying with the local rally director until past midnight, swapping stories over milk shakes at early hours in hotel coffee shops. Once T. W. Wilson got bumped off a plane that had "too many passengers" and had to rent a car. The plane crashed. Bob Cook missed a plane that crashed, and Billy Graham was on a plane that almost met disaster in a Canadian snowstorm. Such incidents merely reinforced their belief that they were God's trailblazers.

They crisscrossed the U.S. and Canada in DC-3s. Billy Graham—no longer an unknown quantity—was the busiest of all, flying 135,000 miles in 1945, and cited as United Airlines' top civilian passenger. In '45 and '46 Billy preached in forty-seven of the forty-eight states and throughout Canada. When a Fort Wayne, Indiana, photographer snapped his picture, he quipped, "Send it to my wife. That's all she sees of me."

Billy found an unusually young * YFC director in Chatham, Ontario. He promptly enlisted 16-year-old Leighton Ford for Wheaton College "where I have a sister." Young Ford did later enroll in Wheaton, married Jean Graham, and is now his brother-in-law's right-hand man.

Billy, Wheelbarrows, and "T" (T. W. Wilson)—everybody in YFC went by first names, still a custom—developed a close, easy fellowship. Billy and Cliff had known each other since having been introduced by newspaperman James Adair in Asheville, North Carolina. Billy and T had grown up together.

Billy had recruited T for YFC, pulling him out of a Georgia pastorate and putting him on the rally trail. On their first cross-country trip together, their plane stopped for refueling in El Paso. The waitress who came to serve them in a restaurant looked at T in his black-and-white checkered suit for several seconds, then asked in a tremulous voice, "What's your name?"

Billy grinned. "Go ahead and tell her, Bob."

The waitress' eyes widened. "You *are* Bob Hope!"

T sputtered, "Who, me? I'm just a country preacher."

*The youngest on record was 15-year-old Gordon McLean, director in Victoria, British Columbia. He is still in YFC.

"No, you're just putting me on," she said thrusting out a menu. "Please autograph this for me, Mr. Hope."

By this time others were crowding around, extending menus and pieces of paper. And as Billy Graham now tells the story, T dutifully signed each one, "Bob Hope—Romans 8:28."

Another time Wheelbarrows and T were in a Chicago hotel room waiting for Billy to return from a late engagement. They doctored Billy's bed, then retired to await his arrival.

After he unlocked the door and entered, they lay quietly while he donned pajamas. But when the bed collapsed under Billy, Wheelbarrows, sleeping on a rollaway fold-up bed, could not contain himself and guffawed.

Billy leaped across the room and sandwiched Wheelbarrows in the fold-up bed. Cliff wriggled free and threw a shoe at Billy. The shoe missed its target and knocked down a mirror onto a can of shaving cream which burst, spraying lather all around the room. From such horseplay and camaraderie developed what T. W. Wilson now calls the "closer-than-brothers" relationship on the Billy Graham team.

However, the field men spent most of their time on serious business. They preached "as unto dying men" and gave fervent come-forward-and-give-Christ-your-heart invitations before jammed rallies. They helped concerned laymen (usually Gideons and members of the Christian Business Men's Committee) and pastors set up boards, rent auditoriums, prepare publicity, and start rallies. They made sure each board had broad representation from local "Bible-believing, Christ-honoring" churches. They checked out prospective rally directors for "soundness of doctrine" and "good character."

And the field men had to pick up the pieces behind more than one YFC rally director who had left town in the middle of the night.

In those booming days a man blessed with a pleasing voice, an "Ipana" smile, merry eyes, a brace of bright-colored neckties, and a well-marked King James Bible could roll into most any town and find a few eager-eyed laymen panting for the souls of youth. By dropping names of nationally known YFC men and reciting the right clichés, he could start a red-hot Saturday night rally while local pastors held their public tongues for fear of losing the most earnest members of their congregations. Then when a scandal erupted and creditors began comparing figures or the local board became snoopy, the man could skip town leaving a permanent smudge across the name YFC. The marvel is that there were so few "gospel gangsters." More problems came from zealous, sincere young men who let zeal for promotion or desire for the opposite sex run ahead of common sense. But whether left behind by frauds or fools, the mess was always sticky for the field men to clean up.

While the YFCI men had been crisscrossing the U.S. and Canada, requests for help from overseas had piled up. The postwar spirit had sent organizations and associations of all sorts around the world to rebuild and restore devastated countries. YFC was among them. Hubert Mitchell, the ex-missionary director in Los Angeles, urged the sending of "sparks, not missionaries, to help Christians in other countries start their own rallies."

Many people across the country were deeply disturbed at the world situation in the spring of 1946. Not too many months before they had danced in the streets over victory. Now it seemed they were headed for a confrontation with Russia. Europe faced critical postwar problems when Torrey, Billy, Chuck Templeton and singer Strat Shufelt volunteered to go. After farewell rallies in Chicago, Charlotte, and Detroit (where sixteen thousand heard Billy and a thousand came forward), the four boarded a plane for England on March 18, 1946. Wesley Hartzell went along to cover the excursion for the William Randolph Hearst newspapers.

Bad weather forced them to lay over at the American Air Force base in Newfoundland where the base social director sized up Torrey as the leader of a vaudeville show and asked for a performance. Not one to pass up an opportunity, Torrey agreed.

Templeton's jokes and Shufelt's Negro spirituals brought cheers and whistles from the packed house. But when Torrey came out, the servicemen began howling, "Bring on the girls. Show us some legs." Shufelt sang again, then Torrey threw Billy to the restless, wolfish soldiers. Billy's apology and testimony didn't quiet them. The angry base commander would have thrown them all in cells, except for reporter Hartzell's plea.

In forty-six days they traveled twenty thousand miles and held

Left: Cliff Barrows leads singing at a send-off rally for YFC's first postwar European missionary team.

Below: Billy Graham, YFC's best known evangelist, flew 135,000 miles in 1945. To a photographer who snapped his picture he quipped, "Send it to my wife. That's all she sees of me."

Above: YFC "ambassadors" pray before takeoff. Left to right: Chuck Templeton, Graham, Strat Shufelt, Torrey Johnson. (CHICAGO DAILY NEWS photo)

Right: March 18, 1946. The team waves goodbye to the crowd.

101 meetings, preaching in churches, auditoriums and from a box at Speaker's Corner in London's Hyde Park. Between engagements they talked theology and methodology with ministers and laymen and among themselves.

At the convention of 700 delegates at Medicine Lake, Minnesota, in the summer of '46, Billy reported on his travels for the past year ("during which I saw my new baby only eight days"). "I believe we are on the verge of a nationwide youth revival," he claimed, but noted a "rising tide of opposition from certain fundamental groups. Why? Because YFC at the moment is doing a job for the Lord Jesus Christ. Because of the 'green eye' they will not back it; they will not have a part in it. But as for me," he said, "I am more sold on YFC than ever before."

Reports from around the country supported Billy's confidence. From all directions came word of a large increase in the number of rallies. Two leadership training schools in the Kansas City area had been the big factor in starting thirty-one new rallies.

Al Metsker, the newly elected regional veep from Kansas City, told the delegates, "Our rally has the highest percentage of youngsters of any rally in the nation." Many grinned knowingly; a few rallies had been classified as "old folks for God" because of the number of adults attending.

While Billy and Torrey were recounting their European trip, two Italian-American brothers excitedly soaked up every word. Phil and Louis Palermo had already been singing and playing in meetings around the Midwest for ten years. They were born of immigrant parents, and grew up in a Chicago suburb with six other brothers and a sister. Through an uncle the entire family was converted to "the new religion."

It was because of prayer meetings in their home that Mom Palermo bought an old organ, then a piano. Louie, the older brother, taught himself to play, then taught Phil. Guitar, banjo, mandolin, other instruments followed, and the singing Palermos were on their way to a ministry which, in the next thirty years, would carry them into dozens of countries.

Before the Medicine Lake convention * finished, they had

*The Medicine Lake delegates voted a dual office structure that continues today. On one side were the regional vice-presidents who were responsible to and for found a chance to talk to Torrey and Billy about their dream.

"Go to Italy under the Youth for Christ banner? Great idea," encouraged Torrey. Then, characteristically, he went on. "We have a policy in YFC that whenever a team goes overseas, they must raise their own support and finance."

The Palermos raised it, and by fall they were ready to go. After farewell rallies in Minneapolis, Detroit, and New York, they made one stopover in London, then touched down in the land their parents had left forty years before.

In the next few months they traveled the length of the country —Sicily, Rome, Naples, Florence, Genoa—holding Youth for Christ meetings, singing, preaching, winning people to Jesus Christ and just plain overwhelming hundreds of Italians.

In Naples, the city mayor appeared at the meeting and said, "What Naples and all of Italy needs is the program of Youth for Christ."

During one meeting in Naples a young priest walked in and sat close to the front. The brothers, not knowing whether to tremble or rejoice, delivered the entire program right down to the invitation. Then who should come forward but the priest. They talked long and hard that evening and the priest, as he said later, "became a new creature in Christ."

Billy Graham returned to England in October, taking only Cliff Barrows to direct music. Tales of YFC sensationalism and showmanship preceded them; some stories circulated that "young Mr. Graham" was bringing back a circus horse and a sword swallower (Barrows)! But they toned down their dress and platform manners and soon convinced skeptical clergymen that a greater power than personal magnetism was with them.

During the bitterly cold winter of '47, while they were in London, Cliff and Billy, along with Bob Evans, stayed at the Cumberland Hotel. One night, in order to keep warm, they put their coats, along with the rugs from the floor and the drapes

---

their respective regions. On the other side were the corporate officers and Board of Directors with Torrey, re-elected as president; Billy, executive vice-president at large (meaning he was the top crowd getter on the rally circuit); Dick Harvey, first vice-president; Bob Pierce, vice-president; Walter Block and George Wilson re-elected treasurer and secretary respectively; and Bill Bond and Chuck Templeton, as two additional board members.

from the windows, on the bed. They had had a meeting in Reading the night before and the response to it was not what they felt it should have been. In the middle of the night Bob awoke to find Billy in pajamas, pacing the floor and praying. Only with some arguing could he persuade Billy to come and pray under the bedclothes where it was warm.

They toured twenty-seven cities and towns, and held 360 meetings in those six months. The windup came in Birmingham with a conference of 250 youth leaders which Graham had called. And the British, as Billy's biographer put it, "caught a gleam which could pierce war-weariness and the defeatism . . . which had settled on much of British religion." *

More YFC sparks for world evangelism flew elsewhere. Spencer DeJong and Don DeVos, both of Dutch descent, along with musician Doug Fisher, landed in Holland and were greeted as heroes by a people grateful for American deliverance from Nazi terror.

Everywhere the YFC men went they filled halls, churches, tents, and saw decisions for Jesus Christ—50, 100, 150—night after night. It was true in the Far East as well as Europe. Men and women who had lost confidence in man's ability to chart his own course, and who were both physically and spiritually hungry, responded to the Gospel.

The results encouraged YFC leaders. Torrey flew to Berlin and conferred with German leaders, hoping to find ways of spreading YFC behind the Iron Curtain, but with no success. One evening, however, as he sat in his hotel room, the idea came for a World Congress on Evangelism. The sparks from America couldn't evangelize the world in one generation by their barnstorming trips. But if they and evangelism-minded Christians from all over the world could come together in one place to pray and plan, a conflagration might be kindled that would spread over the globe. He flew back to Chicago to get the ball rolling.

Watson Argue and Frank Phillips flew south for rallies in Jamaica, Cuba, Venezuela, Brazil, and Argentina. Two thousand squeezed into a 1,300-capacity building in Rio with more left

*J. C. Pollock, *Billy Graham, The Authorized Biography* (New York: McGraw-Hill, 1966).

trying to get in. In Buenos Aires the North Americans saw seas of faces peering through windows.

A young man with an intense zest for life, Bob Pierce, headed for India. With Hubert Mitchell and Dave Morken he swept through the populous nation, which was rejoicing over the end of British colonial rule. Inspired by these three men, Cyril Thompson, a young pastor, hit the rally-organizing trail through the whole country, while Pierce, Mitchell, and Morken moved on to China and preached to unprecedented crowds. From China, rent by civil war, they wrote home that the advancing revolutionaries were not agrarian reformers (as some American officials thought) but dedicated Communists. Mao's motto, they noted, was: "First we nod our heads, then we shake our heads, then we cut off their heads."

The YFCI Convention met again in Winona in 1947. Torrey, re-elected president for a third term, announced that the international office was "in touch" with 800 rallies in North America and that only Nevada of the then forty-eight states did not have YFC. Billy Graham, chairman of the World Progress Committee, reported YFC had gone to forty-six countries during the past year and called for a "gospel invasion" abroad. T. L. Livermore, director of British YFC, reinforced Billy's appeal: "We in Britain do not have men like Billy Graham who can put the Gospel across at 220 words a minute and mow them all down with a spiritual machine gun."

Young preachers left college and seminary to join veterans of the past year in the airlift. Included with the few who came from large Protestant denominations were Jess Moody and Bob Randall from the Southern Baptists' Baylor University. Moody and Randall ignored the jibes of more provincial Southern Baptists that they were "joining up with the Yankees." From the start Southern Baptists had primly ignored YFC in their journals, but not in methodology. Texas Baptists promoted weekly "Adventurers for Christ" youth rallies in churches and spearheaded a Baptist youth revival movement that spread throughout the old South in the late forties and early fifties. Howard Butt, the best-known Southern Baptist youth preacher, subsequently admitted that YFC had inspired the Southern movement.

Europe had just passed a vicious winter. Thousands huddled

hungry and shivering in fuelless homes. On top of that the economy was collapsing and millions faced starvation. American conscience responded with the Marshall Plan and $17 billion of economic aid. The YFC delegates at Winona responded by authorizing $430,000 for twenty evangelistic teams, Bibles, Christian literature. They also shipped food and clothing gathered by North American rallies.

In most foreign cities teams were still well received. But national hosts, who had to live frugally in a war-ravaged economy, were irked by some men who, upon landing, issued requests for "a room with bath in the best hotel."

And some encountered hotel prostitutes who came down the corridors knocking on doors. In one hotel two straight-faced team members sent a "job seeker" to another's door, then hid to watch him blush. But perhaps the most embarrassed was a team "photographer" who, after snapping hundreds of pictures, discovered he had not removed the lens cover!

Promotion hummed at the fourth YFCI Convention at Winona for the scheduled first Congress of World Evangelism in Switzerland just a month away. Most of the "Gospel Invaders" were back. Bob Cook, the Philippines' Gregorio Tinson, and singer-composer Merrill Dunlop returned and reported astonishing success in Japan. "If we don't evangelize Japan today," Cook said, "we shall certainly have to fight her again in some dark tomorrow." Bob Pierce and Ken Anderson cabled from China that they were "winning a thousand souls a day" while barely staying a step ahead of advancing Communists who were "mutilating the bodies of Christians."

With world evangelization fever at its highest pitch ever in YFCI ranks, Torrey jolted the delegates by asking "not to be renominated for president" so he "could travel more in evangelism." Had he not made this request, he would certainly have been elected again, although a few had been complaining about his "high spending" and "domineering ways."

He recommended Bob Cook—a witty and personable preacher and good organizer. Cook was popular. That he was a graduate of Moody, Wheaton, Eastern Baptist Seminary, and held an honorary doctorate from Bob Jones University meant he could appeal to a large number of YFC men who had attended one of these schools. That Bob was Torrey's brother-in-law brought cries of nepotism from some and the allegation that Torrey wanted to be a roving evangelist while keeping control of YFC through his relative.

The convention ended with a near rift, plus a wave of criticism of shallow evangelism with inadequate follow-up. Many directors left Winona saying, "The honeymoon is over. We've got to find new ways to reach young people."

3

Something on the Counters

World attention focused on Berlin in the summer of 1948. Allied planes since late June had been hauling thousands of tons of food and fuel a day to the city under blockade by the Russians. Freedom hung in the balance.

If any headlines were left for religious news, they were generally given to the formation assembly of the World Council of Churches about to convene in Amsterdam. Few noted what many later called one of the most significant evangelical gatherings of the twentieth century—the first Congress on World Evangelization, which YFC sponsored in Beatenburg, Switzerland.

In August, Torrey, Bob, Billy and a plane-load of others left for the six-day conference. The registration list read like a who's who in evangelical circles—Bob Jones, Jr., Stephen W. Payne, Harold Ockenga, Paul Freed, Bob Pierce, Merv Rosell . . . .

Dr. Oswald J. Smith told the 230 delegates from North America, Europe, and the Orient, "Youth for Christ is founded not on a man, nor on a doctrine nor on an organization, but on evangelism—the need of every country. God has raised it up for this hour."

Fresh from embattled China, Bob Pierce and Hubert Mitchell poured fuel on the fires of urgency already burning. Pierce described "the rich harvest of souls being reaped in China," but warned that "doors were fast closing." Four European DPs wearing all the clothing they possessed, moved the delegates to tears and vows of increased relief shipments, as they related

The registration list of the YFC-sponsored first World Congress on Evangelism read like a world evangelical Who's Who. Billy Graham and Torrey Johnson are in the second row, center. (PHOTO STEINHAUER, Interlaken)

their victory of faith amidst suffering, privation, and hunger.

Dawson Trotman, founder of The Navigators, and already involved in YFC follow-up, challenged the delegates to "produce spiritual reproducers." After Trotman's challenge, Billy Graham, Bob Evans, and Hubert Mitchell took Trotman aside for an afternoon of prayer and discussion. Billy, particularly, was concerned that so many YFC converts were slipping through the net.

The Congress brochure challenged men to "go from the Alpine heights of Beatenburg down to the world of men . . . to a new and greater insight into the task of world evangelization. . . ." Significantly, many did. Beatenburg marked the expansion not only of YFC into the world, but of other ministries as well. This was the place many Americans received an international vision, and from Beatenburg YFC hardened into national movements.

Bob Evans had returned to Europe and set up the details of the Congress. He had gone into country after country setting up national committees. The Iron Curtain was still open wide enough to permit him to set up a Polish YFC committee, and delegates from Poland and Hungary came to Beatenburg.

When the Congress closed, the fired-up delegates fanned out across Europe. Torrey preached in the arena in Nimes, France, where Christian martyrs had once been thrown to the lions. Fifty meetings were staged in Germany and Poland. The Palermos returned to Italy, taking Oswald Smith with them.

In Rome local organizers had obtained permission and paid taxes for thousands of rally invitations to be dropped by plane, and had secured the Collegio Romano, the alma mater of Pope Pius, as a meeting place. No doubt the authorities didn't know YFC was a Protestant group but when zealous Catholics learned the true nature of YFC, they protested. To complicate things some of the gospel "bombs" fell on the Vatican—which the authorities had warned was a separate state.

Hours later word came from the president of the Collegio that under no circumstances could they hold their rally there that night. They were stunned—and while they pondered the problem, rumors of possible violence came to them. There were only two things to do—pray and call the American embassy. So while the Palermos talked to God, Bob Evans talked to the military attaché at the embassy. In short time the way was clear for the meeting.

The atmosphere was tense that night. Outside the hall mobs of militant priests and students gathered at the gates of the school, chanting *Viva il Papa*. As the boys sang and Oswald Smith preached, Evans paced back and forth between the hall and the crowd outside (where the military attaché kept a watchful eye). But the meeting went on and before the evening was over, some two hundred and fifty people had professed Christ as their Saviour.

The following months brought new anxieties to Americans at home. Peace in Europe and the Far East had been secured at a high price. Fears of Communist encroachment had been mollified in 1945 when Eisenhower returned saying that the Russians sincerely wanted U.S. friendship. But he quickly changed his mind when Soviet troops began stripping eastern Europe of physical goods and freedoms and, as Churchill described it, an "iron curtain" descended on Europe. When, in September, 1949, Truman's press secretary announced to startled reporters that the Russians had the A-bomb, security became the watchword for

YFC "big four" of the early '50s. Left to right: Hubert Mitchell, secretary for world evangelism; Bob Cook, president; Billy Graham, vice-president; Ted Engstrom, executive director.

millions of Americans. Men were willing to pay any price to stem the tide. The CIA was created and the National Security Act passed. Widespread suspicion of Communist infiltration reflected the strain under which the country labored.

It seemed to some that YFC also strained to keep momentum in the movement. Critics on the left and on the right nibbled at the edges and cautiously watched the new president to see which way he would move. In Chicago 36-year-old Bob Cook surprised some people by proving that he was his own man. He shrewdly realized that the movement couldn't keep running on a high head of steam generated by a thousand or so evangelical entrepreneurs, too many of whom skated on the thin ice of panic financing and high-powered promotion. He began laying down guidelines and needling rally directors who weren't measuring up.

Finances got top priority. "Let's get away from this business of having to tell people, 'Please help us! We're just about to fold up,' " he said. "Let's base our appeal on solid projects and new and better techniques. Let's build public confidence where people will give willingly without thinking there's a racket to YFC."

Bob deplored the "talented opportunist who was in YFC for

self-interest, the professional religious entertainer, the evangelist who lived in expensive hotels on the offerings of poor saints who wanted to help young people, the fast-buck artist who skipped town leaving the local board with a pile of bills. My heart burden for YFC is that every sham and phoney note shall be taken out," he said at Winona in '51. "We were born in miracle—why degenerate into fraud? To this end I pledge myself to seek God daily, to be a man of God; to urge leaders everywhere to put prayer, souls, holiness of life, and missions first."

Harnessing independent-minded rally directors who rebelled at the slightest sign of central control was no easy task. Bob kept a sharp eye on men who paid little heed to business principles or snuggled up to one element of the evangelical community while snubbing the rest. He wanted to eliminate the bad marks by putting more "teeth" in the YFC chartering program. "Are we forming only a roost for nondescript individualistic birds?" he asked.

The ebullient Bob Cook was YFC's best recruiter and motivator at a time when there was no organized personnel procurement program. He could fire up a young preacher who was trying to decide between the insecurity of a YFC directorship and a more promising denominational pastorate. For Bob there was no ministry more relevant to the times, more crucial to the future of the church than youth evangelism. And since few churches were doing anything in the field, other than maintaining their own Sunday schools, this meant YFC.

A visit to Regina, Saskatchewan, where a local board had just appointed 18-year-old Russ Reid director, illustrates how Cook felt. He grasped the young Canadian's hand and boomed, "This is the greatest day of your life, Russell. Don't you ever forget it." Young Russ didn't. The following summer he went out and started thirty rallies throughout the province.

Bob quickly saw a need for orienting new directors fresh from school, the pastorate, or business. But regional veep Al Metsker in Kansas City had thought of it first and was conducting a training school in his area. Bob simply persuaded the YFCI board to utilize Metsker's program and facilities for the entire constituency.

The first YFCI Leadership Training School convened in Kansas City, September 7, 1954. Lanky Carl "Kelly" Bihl, former rally director in Toledo and a new YFCI staff evangelist, directed the school which touched on fifty-one subjects in two weeks, ranging from how to get along with pastors to how to counsel with juvenile delinquents.*

As a traveling president, Cook maintained a hectic pace. "Whenever I come to a town, I am met at the train or plane by the local leader who rolls out the red carpet. He has the committee there and the photographer. He gives me the glad hand, we go and have supper, and I preach to the committee. I get in his car and we go to the rally. I preach and after that he takes me to his home or to a hotel, and we talk until two in the morning. I stagger to bed, get up the next day and start all over again."

Directors who put up an everything-is-going-great front were sometimes jolted by Bob's analysis. He didn't mind telling a man in private that he needed to make some adjustments. By 1951 Bob was convinced that the one-shot rally approach was in serious trouble in many cities.

"Some of us," he said, "are holding desperately to a fumbling, stumbling, crumbling rally deal when we could be shaking the community for God, reaching high schoolers, reaching servicemen, carrying on missionary work and projects around the globe! The rally idea is sound but in most places the . . . rally is just the show window. Let's get something on the counters the rest of the week. Let's get going!"

Bible clubbing was the biggest and best piece of merchandise that got on the YFC counters during the fifties. It was to YFC in the fifties what the rally had been in the forties.

Religious educators had been moaning over the Biblical illiteracy of both churched and non-churched youth. One survey taken among 18,434 high schoolers in southern states at the close of World War II showed that 16,000 could not name three major prophets; 12,000, the four Gospels; and 10,000, three of the twelve apostles. The information revealed by this and other

*Only two of the thirty students in this first school are with YFC to date. Bill Eakin, executive coordinator, Metropolitan (New York) YFC; Don Whipple, director of Greater Minneapolis YFC.

similar surveys, plus the dropping of Bible reading and prayer from many public schools, helped create a climate receptive to starting Bible clubs.

But again, as with leadership training, Kansas City YFC already had something going. The impetus for starting YFC clubs came from high schooler Judy Raby after she attended a Winona Lake convention. Judy suggested the idea to Al Metsker who, busy with other work, said, "Go talk to school officials and come back and see me before school starts." Judy went straight to Dr. Herold C. Hunt, then superintendent of Kansas City schools, and got his permission to start a club.

By the end of the next school term Kansas City had not one but twelve thriving "Youth on the Beam" clubs meeting on school property before and after school.

Metsker told Judy (now a foreign missionary), "We've got something here, but we need help." Help came in the form of a dashing, dark-haired ex-mechanic named Jack Hamilton who joined Metsker's staff in 1946 to coordinate the club program.

Jack got excited fast about the world-wide future of high school Bible clubs when he went to Winona '47 (on borrowed money) and watched kids listen and sometimes squirm under the preaching of Torrey Johnson, Billy Graham, and other crowd inspirers. It wasn't enough to get kids "under the sound of Gospel preaching," he felt. They needed to study the Bible for themselves and put it into practice on the campus. Bible clubs were doing this in Kansas City; why not in every YFC city?

The Kansas City club director knew that YFC men had more ideas than there were "thees" and "thous" in the King James Bible. They would be more likely to listen to the club idea if he could show Kansas City as a model, so Jack and his wife Mary Jeanne set up Bible quiz programs and talent contests in the twelve clubs with competition between schools staged at the Saturday night rallies. In two years the Hamiltons took almost every club member through the New Testament in a series of quizzes.

In the summer of '49, Hamilton and Metsker went to Winona, determined to sell the club program. The quizzing idea immediately caught fire as directors saw it as an added attraction for their rallies. Soon Bob Cook was calling "high school Bible club work the next great gospel frontier* . . . highlighted and made more strategic by the fact that atomic warfare will most certainly finish off millions of these youngsters before routine evangelism gets around to them." Jack Hamilton was lifted from Kansas City to travel and promote the program. Don Lonie, a prankish Moody and Wheaton grad who had worked with the Chicago Hi-C clubs, was appointed Jack's assistant.

Hamilton and Lonie were each personalities in their own right. Jack loved to wear garish shirts and ties and he drove a red convertible—the gift of a YFC supporter. Lonie was gifted with an acid wit that the kids lapped up when he began cutting down both teenage and adult hypocrisies. Though no arm-waving windmill in the pulpit, Lonie never hesitated to speak bluntly. Russ Reid, now a publishing and advertising executive, still remembers the day in Vancouver when Lonie called him an idiot for dropping out of school. Reid was so shocked he went back to school to prove to Lonie that he wasn't an idiot.

"Lonie stories" soon began circulating on the YFC circuit. One had him splicing a Mickey Mouse cartoon into a missionary film when he was a student at Moody Bible Institute. Another credited him with having a case of beer sent over to a Wheaton College board of directors' meeting.

Hamilton and Lonie not only enthused kids about starting Bible clubs in their schools, they easily won support from parents and pastors who were frustrated by the action of the Supreme Court. At every stop in a U.S. rally city, Hamilton said, "The Court is taking the Bible out of the high schools. With Bible clubs we can put it back in through the lives of young people on fire for God."

The club movement snowballed and by October, 1950, every high school in one populous California county had a club. By the end of the school year 700 clubs had been started by YFC directors; by March, 1952, when *Time's* Henry Luce observed "a more serious interest in religion in America than in thirty years," the number passed the 1,000 mark; by Winona '55, the YFCI office recorded 1,956 clubs.

*In Chicago Hi-C clubs met in homes after school. Before this a few Bible clubs functioned off and on around the country; Billy Graham had one at his Sharon High School near Charlotte, North Carolina, in 1936.

Sometimes the testimony of one club would touch the heart of a town. A doctor's daughter in Worland, Wyoming, wrote to Jack Hamilton asking him to start a club to "reach the unsaved kids" in her town. Jack replied: "Start a prayer meeting—and go to the YFCI convention at Winona Lake."

Sue Anderson went to Winona and things began to happen. When YFC state director Franklin Robbie came to Worland he accidentally discovered a prayer list made up by Sue with twelve names. Following several names was scrawled "Praise the Lord." These had been won to Christ. On the list were the top football players on the Worland team.

Sue's prayer meeting grew and in a few months the teens in it asked school authorities for a room for a YFC club. Permission was granted and soon forty or fifty teens were meeting regularly at Washakie High.

Robbie noted the activity—and the enthusiasm of local laymen and pastors—and wrote to Wendy Collins, then in Finland as captain of a YFC team. By Easter Collins was installed as a full-time director for the area and rallies were running regularly.

Sue graduated from Washakie and went to Bob Jones University. One Friday night, a year after the club began, a dozen members of the Worland football team gathered at her home. It was the night before the state class A championship, and Sue's dad, the team physician, had brought them together for a pre-game prayer meeting.

"Lord, we'd like to win tomorrow," one prayed, "but . . . win or lose, help us to play like real Christians."

The next afternoon they defeated Douglas 26-13 and that night they lined the platform at the YFC rally to give testimonies. Halfback Dick Harkins, who scored all four touchdowns, was home sick, but Bill Carle read his testimony for him: "I was on the wrong road, but a sermon by Merv Rosell changed my way."

The other halfback, Larry McGarvin, spoke up, "I've lived in the Lord's family for about one year and I wouldn't trade it for anything."

Right end Jerry Smotherton didn't give a testimony that night. It wasn't until after the meeting behind the platform that he knelt and took Christ as his Saviour. But two days later he did add his opinion.

"I've been a Christian for only two days now and in these two days I've surely learned some of the blessings. . . . Being a Christian is more than going to church . . . it's letting the Lord come into my heart, letting him help me and guide me."

Enthusiastic letters of appreciation came to Robbie from the superintendent of schools and from the school football coach. The YFC magazine did a story on Worland and called it "God's Western Workshop." And it all began when one high-school girl wrote and asked about a YFC club.

Everybody in YFC liked the clubs. They boosted attendance in sagging Saturday night rallies. They defused pastors' complaints that YFC was imitating church services. They gave high schoolers the opportunity to participate in programs, be on quiz teams, and display other talent. They offered an ecumenical security blanket for Christian kids from conservative churches who felt lonely and discouraged in the schools.

The mark of a consecrated clubber became the King James Bible on top of his books, with the latest YFC magazine directly underneath. This—supported by silent target prayers at every bell ringing—was supposed to open opportunities for witnessing. Example: When one clubber dropped her Bible, a classmate asked, "What course is that?" "Life," she replied and then began to quote Bible verses about life in the spiritual dimension.

Don Lonie is credited with coining the phrase, "Every Bible ought to be *read*." A profit-minded Bible publisher began turning out red-covered YFC-stamped Bibles by the thousands. Rally directors and their visiting evangelists preached from red Bibles. (Every member of Billy Graham's team carried one.) Evangelical laymen and pastors fell into line and for awhile it looked as if black Bibles might be relegated to funeral homes. Naturally, every clubber filled the flyleaf under the red cover with autographs and favorite Scripture verses from YFC preachers and musicians. Girls especially liked to show their autographs when classmates displayed the scribbling of "worldly" show-business celebrities.

Most clubs met at first on school property—in empty classrooms, gyms, lunchrooms, etc.—before and after school. But in '52 and '53 skittish superintendents, fearful of bucking the Supreme Court, began cracking down. Some school administrators did permit the clubs to continue meeting on school property, usually because they understood the interdenominational sponsorship and purpose of the clubs. Principal Benjamin Weiss of the 6,000-student Metropolitan High School in Los Angeles, himself a YFC board member, persuaded his city school board that the clubs were not in violation of the Supreme Court's dictum.

Kansas City didn't fare so well. When the order came denying the use of school property, Metsker met the crisis by buying the first in a fleet of "Youth on the Beam" buses. A club director drove the bus from school to school, parking just long enough for meetings, and on Saturday night the bus carried kids to the rally.

The Bible quiz mania grew alongside and was aided by clubs. Kansas City, the originators, not surprisingly walked off with the honors in the first two national contests held at Winona in 1949 and 1950.*

When Hamilton became national club director, he spread the fever. Soon school teams competed against each other, city champs challenged other cities and rally all-stars fought their way through state and area competition to the international finals at Winona Lake. Before long twenty thousand teens a year were involved in quizzing.

Picture this scene on the platform of the Billy Sunday Tabernacle at Winona Lake. A slender young man in a gold blazer speaks one word—neither a command nor warning. Yet as he speaks, ten teenagers instantly freeze in concentration. Not a muscle moves; breathing slows perceptibly. In a semi-crouched position they sit on the edge of their chairs waiting for the first key word to trigger a mental, then a physical reaction which will shoot them, arms flying, into the air.

The quizmaster (for many years, Hamilton) had simply said,

*Winona quiz winners since 1950: Detroit, '51 and '52; Los Angeles, '53 and '54; West Suburban Chicago, '55 and '56; Northwest Virginia (Washington, D. C. suburbs), '58; St. Louis, '59; Mississippi Valley (Quad Cities of Iowa and Illinois on the Mississippi River), '60; St. Louis, '61; Minneapolis, '62; San Diego, '63; Southeast Kentucky, '64; Fox Valley, Illinois, '65, '66; Washington County, Pennsylvania, '67; Marion, Indiana, '68; Hampstead, Md., '69. No team has ever won more than twice.

Every rally had a theme. This one may have been "repentance."

Center: Funspirations were big in the early years and always ended in a salvation challenge. Today's "big bashes," under new names and with open discussion as an added feature, serve the same goals.

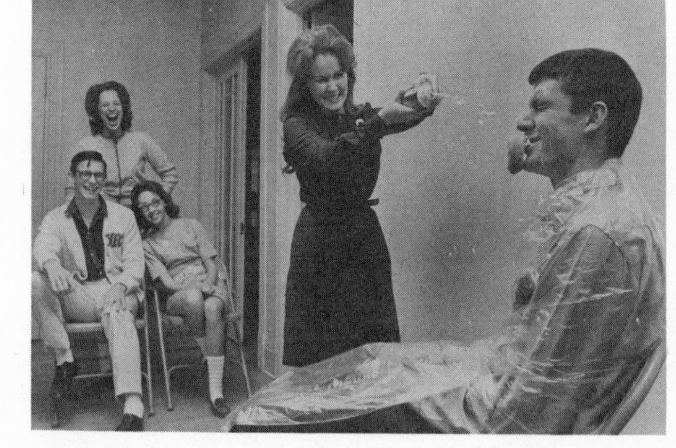

Below: YFC club meeting in St. Louis. Clubs at first typically had a majority of girls. Today attendance is more equally balanced between the sexes.

Bible quizzing
reached its heyday in the '50s.
Excitement built with every question.

Center:
Quiz team finals at Winona.
Under the rules, the first person
off the chair got to finish
the question, then answer it.
Kids often jumped after only
one word was spoken, even though
questions were drawn from
an entire Gospel or
several epistles.

Right:
Quizzing was still
going strong in the '60s.
Pictured are the San Diego
national winners for 1963
with their trophy.

"Question." And the two teams waited for the first Bible question. When it came, however, five quizzers jumped in perfect unison before the quizmaster could speak more than three words. Above their heads an electronic scoreboard glowed, and a light indicated which teenager was up first. The contestant walked to the microphone, completed the question the quizmaster had begun, then answered it.

When the quizzing fever struck, teens thought of little else. They memorized entire books of the Bible, organized cheering sections, and donned sometimes clever but often outlandish costumes. Rally directors smiled at the trappings that grew up around quizzing, but as they watched they knew they had a handle on the problem of getting teenagers to read the Bible. Something happened to a teen who spent hundreds of hours with his nose in the Word.

A gospel team member wrote back from Europe, "Through quizzing I found that the Bible related to my life. . . . I saw that the Bible had more than a plan of salvation but a plan for my Christian life as well."

Years after her quizzing days, a pastor's wife commented, "I memorized seven books of the Bible, and once I got a taste for learning the Scriptures through quizzing, I just couldn't stop."

Intensive Bible study, day after day, week after week saw results years after the quizzers put away their uniforms. A soldier wrote that often when he faced temptation, a verse of Scripture he had learned while quizzing would come to mind.

Knowing the answer alone was not enough to make a champion quizzer. Most teams, if given written exams, would score 100 percent. It required both mind and muscle, and teams began rigorous physical exercises to develop agility. Some weighted themselves down with rocks. Others practiced jumping off curbs to strengthen leg muscles. Most kept a close watch on diet.

Besides keeping them physically fit, hundreds of teenagers found that Bible quizzing did something for them in school. "It helped me in a lot of ways," a sophomore said. "I used to hate to study, but because of quizzing I now get A's." A college girl commented, "Since quizzing I can think faster and clearer, reason better and apply my mind to my studies. . . . My average in school went from C to B, and I've received a scholarship. Now I

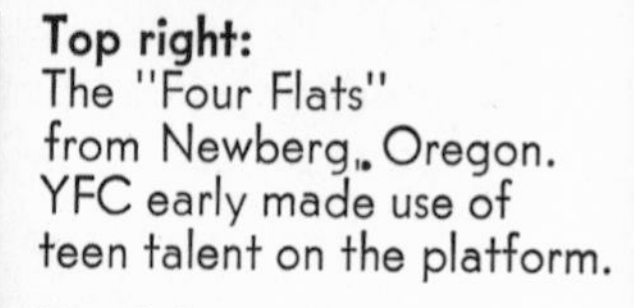

Top right:
The "Four Flats" from Newberg, Oregon. YFC early made use of teen talent on the platform.

Top left:
Talent contests at Winona produced not only musical performers but also teen songleaders and preachers for rallies. Here contestant Marc Billigmeier practices his songleading abilities.

Center left:
A contestant waits behind stage to compete in the national Teen Talent finals.

Center right:
The Isaac family from Canada contributed these winners, and another sister joined a Teen Team.

Bottom:
Lineup at Winona's Eskimo Inn, watering place for tens of thousands of YFC teens for over two decades.

can also speak before a group." And club leaders found that more than one teenager learned his true spiritual condition and gave his life to Christ as he studied the Word.

The talent contests got almost as much attention as the quiz runoffs. Cities sent their most talented teens to compete before the judges for honors as best preacher, song leader, vocalist, instrumentalist, or choir. Categories changed to keep up with music trends. And when YFCI began making films, screen tests were held at Winona to select the best teenage actors and actresses. All in all, YFC at Winona was the best competition for Hollywood that evangelicalism had to offer.

Naturally a few older men on the sidelines regretted the reduction in preaching which accompanied the teen productions. More than one groused, "YFC isn't what it used to be. Before long nobody will be preaching." To such criticism, Cook and his colleagues (all of whom loved to preach) had a ready rejoinder: "So what, if the kids are getting converted and trained? That's what YFC is for."

4

The Spin-Offs

Clubs, quizzing, and talent contests were only the beginning. Spurred by Bob Cook "to go into the highways and byways in unique ministries," the imaginative YFC entrepreneurs started so many programs that headquarters became like the fabled old woman who lived in a shoe. Bob and his associates had so many things going they could hardly keep count.

A new ministry to delinquent youth blossomed after Bob noticed YFC was reaching "comparatively few from the so-called 'seamy side of town.' One reason," he said, "is that so much of our advertising and programs are slanted to happy Christian youngsters. Let's do something to reach the teens outside."

Oakland had anticipated his concern and in 1948 had held a summer camp for teens in trouble. Interest picked up markedly when 17-year-old Gordon McLean, YFC director in Victoria, British Columbia, won two teenage murderers while counseling at nearby Oakalla Prison Farm. The testimonies of the boys made front page stories in Vancouver newspapers.

Los Angeles YFC Director Roy McKeown picked up the cue and in 1950 set up six summer camps for troubled boys under the direction of Louis Zamperini, the nationally known track star converted in Billy Graham's '49 Los Angeles campaign.

Impetus for a Youth Guidance department came in 1952 from the conversion of gang boy Ralph Cavanaugh in Gary, Indiana. Life had bumped Ralph Cavanaugh from one bad home situation to another in Gary in the forties. Trouble was his shadow. By his teen years he was a gang boy, drinking, thieving, concentrating on making himself a community nuisance—which he did quite well.

Not much influence for good touched his early life. As he remembers it, "I once had a deep craving for something, but I didn't know what it was. I used to listen to religious radio programs and I thought religion might help me, but nobody ever explained to me how to go about finding God. I finally made up my mind that religion was for adults and that I'd be better off to forget it until I got older."

When he was older a persistent elderly woman whom he worked for on occasion urged him to attend a YFC rally. He went, but he was bored—by the speaker, the music, the whole thing. At the end of the meeting a man put his hand on Ralph's shoulder and said something about being a Christian. Then, for reasons he couldn't explain, Ralph found himself walking toward the front of the auditorium and to a counseling room.

Ralph described his own feeling, "As I walked that aisle, all of my hardness and disgust and rebellion just melted away; and in the counseling room I received Jesus Christ into my heart as my Lord and Saviour." It was Bruce Love, Gary YFC director, who explained salvation to Ralph that night.

A high-school principal who knew Cavanaugh said, "If religion can do that much for a teenager, I'm all for it." The principal's enthusiasm moved Bruce Love to begin a counseling program at the Gary detention home for juvenile offenders.

Gordon McLean became the first Youth Guidance director for YFCI; Wendy Collins, a Chicagoan who had developed an unusually successful youth work in Wyoming, succeeded him. Wendy changed the name of the department to Lifeline and set up an adoption program where individuals could sponsor a teenager for five dollars a month and receive monthly progress reports.

Clubs, quizzing, talent contests, leadership training schools, and Lifeline were only a few of the plethora of highway and hedge ministries begun during Bob Cook's term as president.

In 1954, the hot rod craze started Bill Price, business manager for the Southwest Pacific region, thinking about a ministry through car clubs. He spilled his idea to Maurice Brockington

These basketball players took part in YFC's Christian Olympics, one of the many spin-offs that proliferated in the '50s. Bob Pierce finally advised YFC's leaders to concentrate on their best specialty—high school evangelism.

in Los Angeles. Maurice rented an old garage, found some wrecked cars and a group of young grease monkeys, and organized the "Boltin' Bishops" for "fellowship for Christian rodders and as a means of winning unsaved rodders to Christ." Not only did they put together cars that almost defied imagination—good vocational training—but they also won boys to Christ who never before had shown interest in anything spiritual. Newspapers ran stories, and more "Boltin' Bishops" clubs began popping up in other cities.

Bob Cook proposed a "Christian Lettermen's Club" at a YFCI Executive Council session "to organize Christian young men on high school and college campuses who have a common liking for athletics and to unite and strengthen the testimony of each of them." This resulted in the first "Christian Olympics" at Winona '54. One of the young athletes participating was Rafer Johnson, recently converted at a YFC club banquet in Fresno, California, and later to become famous in the World Olympics. However, interest in lettermen's clubs never picked up except in Ohio, where a few such clubs function today.

Film and literature ministries had more permanent foundations and support. Principally under Ken Anderson's direction, YFCI in the fifties produced, through Gospel Films, a steady run of pictures utilizing talent selected through screen tests at Winona. The first film, *Counterattack,* brought criticism from conservatives who okayed documentaries but called playing the roles of other characters "hypocritical." Then after story films gained general acceptance, the same crowd jumped YFC for showing Christian films in commercial theaters. "Compromise," they charged, even after hundreds of non-church goers were converted. The respected A. W. Tozer even wrote a booklet on the subject. But he finally admitted to an editor friend, "I have fathered a dud."

The YFC magazine slowly evolved from a house organ to a genuine youth magazine with articles slanted toward teenagers. However, the editors avoided articles on controversial subjects such as civil rights. In those days they couldn't conceive of relating the Negro struggle for integrated facilities to Christianity.

Evangelistic sparks continued to girdle the globe, and in 1951, 170 teams went overseas in "YFC's Million Souls Crusade." They went under the auspices of YFC but raised their own finances. Some teams left with only one-way tickets, "trusting God" that home supporters would see more light and bring them back. Bob Cook called the overseas teams "the spiritual equivalent of the Marshall Plan."

That spring a team of Moody Bible Institute students spent a weekend at the Milwaukee YFC rally where Wendy Collins was director. Reinnie Barth had stopped in Milwaukee that weekend with long stories of ministry in Europe, and Bob Cook was the speaker. Sunday noon as the group gathered for dinner, Cook eyed the Jubilairs and said, "I think your team ought to go to Europe."

The team objected. For one thing, some subjects were given only every other year at MBI. If they missed these they'd have to wait another year to get back in. Then, of course there was the draft. The Korean conflict was on, and if they stepped out of Moody, Uncle Sam might send them across the wrong ocean.

But Cook urged them to talk to the dean. God had spoken to Bob Cook and to the quartet, and now He spoke to the administration at MBI, clearing the way for the team.

After the Winona convention that summer the team* piled into the 1948 Frazer owned by Wendy Collins and headed east. Collins was to be team speaker and his wife, Norma, pianist.

The Frazer was to be their transportation for the next six months—and also their tribulation. Shortly before sailing the overdrive went out, and a Frazer without overdrive was nearly useless. It would have cost $168 to repair it, and $100 was all they had, so they sailed with it as it was.

In Europe they started with meetings in England, Holland, Belgium, France, Germany. But Scandinavia was their target, and the time finally came to head north. The morning they were to leave, when Collins went out to check the car and fill the tank, he noticed a dent in the fender. During the checkout he tried the overdrive (for which the team had been praying regularly). Now it engaged, and it worked perfectly for the rest of the trip.

In four months of ministering in Scandinavia they had had great spiritual results but had saved few funds for the trip home. So they had thousands of copies of their team pictures printed on newsprint and sold them after their concerts. In southern Finland while selling the pictures, they greeted people with a common greeting—peace. At least they thought that was what they were saying. It turned out they had the word confused and were actually asking for money.

It was the Green Dollar (their affectionate name for the Frazer) which finally brought enough money to purchase return tickets, and by February they were all back at Moody.

On the other side of the globe Chiang Kai-shek now welcomed YFC evangelists to his island. China had fallen to the Communists in 1949 and the Nationalist government had been set up in Formosa. Dave Morken, the last YFC man to leave the China mainland, had been held captive by the Communists in Shanghai for several weeks. He, Dick Hillis and others won an estimated thousand converts a week in Formosa for several months. At one time thirty thousand Nationalist Chinese were

*Besides Collins and his wife, the team included Bruce Love (now Fox Valley YFC director), Tedd Bryson (Great Lakes area vice-president for YFCI), Dick Proknow and Will Davis (both currently Illinois pastors).

enrolled in follow-up Bible study, with twenty-three secretaries handling the correspondence.

President Syngman Rhee invited YFC teams into South Korea even before the uneasy truce was signed with Communist North Korea in 1953. Bob Pierce and Ken Anderson hopped about the countryside in helicopters, preaching to prisoners of war, taking films, and weeping over the suffering orphans.

Everett Swanson,* ex-paratrooper Theron "Corky" Farris, and others went to Japan where Soldiers Field convert Kenny Joseph had started the first YFC rally in Osaka. When Farris returned to enter seminary, he told of his experiences from the pulpit and moved deacon-contractor O. K. Bozeman to "go and see for myself." Bozeman saw, returned home, sold out his business and went back as a career missionary.

YFC made a pioneering missionary thrust in 1952 by co-sponsoring with Taylor University the first Venture for Victory basketball team to Southeast Asia for a summer of exhibition games and witnessing. The first team (coached by Don Odle and composed of players from Taylor) spoke to 750,000 people before and after games and during half times, and turned over 17,000 decision cards to missionaries and national churches. Three years later six of the seven first team members were preparing to return as career missionaries.

After the pacesetting meetings in Switzerland (1948) and France (1949), the YFC-sponsored Congress of World Evangelism convened in Brussels, Belgium, in 1950, while rioters swarmed through the streets. In 1952 it was held in Belfast, Ireland, where, after Bob Cook reported YFC activity in seventy-eight countries (meaning a YFC evangelist had stopped at least once during the year), five hundred prayed the night through.

Sam Wolgemuth, a young Brethren in Christ pastor from Waynesboro, Pa., took his family to Japan to set up the 1953 Congress in Tokyo. Thirty-five teams fanned out to hold crusades in forty-four of Japan's forty-five prefectures, and after the Congress ten veteran missionaries apologized for having predicted it would be a fiasco.

*Swanson later started Compassion, Inc., which now cares for more than twenty thousand orphans.

The sixth Congress convened in São Paulo in the summer of 1955. Phil and Louie Palermo, who had missed only one of the first five congresses, were there. As before, gospel teams toured neighboring countries, then gathered again in São Paulo for the chartered flight home. Phil and Louie, weary but, as usual, elated, began to sing "Tenderly He Watches Over Me." "Before we knew it," they recall, "one delegate began to weep." Another told how he believed God was calling him back to Brazil. A prayer meeting convened and spread through the plane, lasting four hours or so. Finally the co-pilot came back and explained, "I'm glad to see you folks praying, but could you scatter your prayer toward the front of the plane? We're losing altitude." For hours the pilot had struggled while the unknowing, rejoicing delegates praised God in the back of the plane.

Bob Cook, meanwhile, had moved YFCI headquarters to Wheaton, a Chicago suburb, and built a president's "cabinet." The character of the staff indicated, as he put it, that "the flamboyance of the past was giving way to animated dignity." It was Cook's answer to the perpetual complaint that YFC was frothy, superficial, sensational and unstable.

Bob took the most direct route in dealing with problems and criticisms. Once in Kansas City, when he saw discussion among field men wasn't easing strained relations, he said, "Okay, fellows, you've made enough speeches. Time to pray." They knelt, but no one prayed aloud. Finally Don Lonie said, "Lord, You know there are a couple of fellows here I wouldn't trust further than I could throw a stick." Whereupon Bob tapped Lonie on the shoulder. "Who are they?" Lonie blurted the names and the prayer meeting got into high gear.

In another tense prayer meeting Bob called for "old-fashioned repentance." Before the praying was over, Lonie—a soft touch for loans—had collected several old debts.

Bob's smiling knack of asking a visitor, "What new thing did you get from the Lord this morning?" or, "How many souls did you win last month?" disarmed more than one angry director who had come for his scalp.

He also invited criticism from pastors suspicious of YFC. Early in his presidency he met, in Los Angeles, the late Dr. Donald Grey Barnhouse, scholarly Presbyterian divine from Philadelphia. When Barnhouse began grousing about YFC, Bob countered, "You're right, Doctor. We have made a lot of mistakes. Come down to our meeting and set us right."

Barnhouse grudgingly came and took the rostrum. "Who ever heard of God speaking through a horse?" he snorted, alluding to the famous trick horse that by this time remained only a past embarrassment to YFC. To this, a voice in the back called, "How about Balaam's ass?" A spasm of laughter overcame Barnhouse, who after awhile was agreeing that YFC's positive contributions outweighed the negative.

Open-minded critics like Barnhouse could be reasoned with; others could not. The radical left differed with YFC on such basic points of theology as the inspiration of Scripture and the necessity of spiritual rebirth. Bob made no attempt to placate them. The radical right attacked almost everything new that came along. Some opposed almost any amusements for teenagers—even girls' basketball games ("nudity") and bowling. Some decried any form of makeup on girls. And President Cook himself sounded off against skating parties as "dancing on wheels."

Less than ten years after the YFC movement became an organization, most of the key old hands had moved on. Torrey, except for occasional rallies and anniversaries, had moved into general evangelism. Roger Malsbary and Richard Harvey had returned to ministries within the Christian and Missionary Alliance.

Many of the men who had jumped on the YFC bandwagon at the close of the war were young men. They never thought of making a career out of YFC. It was the thing God told them to do at the moment and they obeyed. Later they began to ask themselves, "What does God have planned for me? What is to be my life's work?" And, understandably, many spun off to start ministries closely related to what they had been doing in YFC.

Of these, Billy Graham is the most famous. YFCI's first staff evangelist built his own evangelistic team from some of the best timbers in the YFCI structure.

He got business manager George Wilson from Minneapolis YFC. Crusade organizer Walter Smyth came from Philadelphia. Associate evangelists T. W. Wilson and music director Cliff Barrows came from the YFCI field staff. T. W.'s brother, Grady, was a regular YFC speaker. Associate evangelist Leighton Ford (his new brother-in-law) and pianist Tedd Smith came from Canadian YFC. And soloist George Beverly Shea, though never a YFC staff member, had sung for many rallies.

Besides key people, the Billy Graham team got from YFC much of the expertise for holding successful evangelistic crusades. YFC recruited boards composed mainly of laymen from cooperating churches. So did the Graham team. YFC men lined up and recognized delegations from local churches and Christian organizations to help fill auditoriums. So did the Graham team. YFC men (those who listened to Bob Cook) had financial records audited and available for scrutiny. So did the Graham team.

However, in a sense Billy Graham never left YFC. He continued as a board member of YFCI and, until his schedule became too tight, spoke almost every summer at the Winona convention.

Another YFC personality who left for "a wider field of service" —a cliché for explaining why anyone left YFC for other Christian work—was a Westerner who had been one of the forty-two delegates at the first constitutional convention. Bob Pierce had trudged through India and the Far East on evangelistic junkets in the late forties. "He seems to be," someone wrote of him, "one of the few naturally, uncontrollably honest men I have ever met; his prevailing temper is one of enthusiasm and zest for life." On these jaunts misery and physical suffering broke the heart of the man and gave him his first "world vision."

But if Christ had put compassion in Pierce's heart he had also put urgency in his bones. It was impossible for Pierce not to do anything about what he saw. Years later a biographer would watch him board a plane and then write of him, "To Bob this was only another step in the long journey to which he has dedicated his life." For several years he flew back and forth across the Pacific, making documentaries and discovering needs in Korea, then returning to show the films and raise funds in "World Vision" rallies held under YFC auspices.

Though he would give his last five dollars (which he once did, in Korea, saying, "It's only a little, but at least it's something"), some thought he spent money too freely and were pleased when he organized the non-profit World Vision, Inc. As Billy Graham had done, Pierce chose his key associates from YFC ranks, starting with Frank Phillips (World Vision's first vice-president), the director of Portland, Oregon, YFC.*

Meanwhile, in Europe, Bob Evans had a different kind of concern—how to conserve the results of the hundreds of rallies across the continent.

Torrey Johnson had dug Evans out of a Naval training school in Norfolk, where Evans was teaching. He had served in Africa and Italy and finally stopped a piece of German lead in the invasion of southern France. Torrey got the Navy to ship him to Chicago for a patriotic rally; then he hired him to be the first executive director of YFCI.

Evans spent weekdays at the old 130 N. Wells office, booking Billy Graham and the other field men. Then on the weekends he jumped on a plane to head for his own preaching assignment. But it wasn't long before he was back in Europe where he became YFC's key man, setting up meetings and organizing local committees.

There he also tried to help some young Christians get their feet on the ground and arranged for several to go to the States for Bible school training. But he knew that wasn't the real answer. So in 1949 he resigned from Youth for Christ and with six students opened a Bible school in his Paris apartment. Like many others, Evans met criticism and opposition as well as financial problems. Some claimed his training wasn't thorough. Evans persisted. A few years later he founded the Greater Europe Mission, and over the years established Bible schools in Germany, Italy, and Sweden.

Paul Freed, YFC director for Greensboro, North Carolina, also caught a missionary vision while evangelizing overseas for YFC. Missionaries in Morocco begged him to find a way to broadcast the gospel to persecuted national evangelicals in Spain. Freed came home and shared his concern in YFC circles. He raised funds and returned in 1954 to broadcast the first programs of TransWorld Radio from Algiers. When the Moroccan govern-

*Pierce, too, has retained a close relationship and continued to serve on the YFCI board.

ment stopped all private broadcasting, Freed moved TransWorld to Monte Carlo and commandeered a 100,000-watt transmitter that would reach throughout Europe and into Russia. In 1961, from its location on a Caribbean island, TransWorld Radio manned the first superpowered (over 750,000 watts) missionary radio station in the world. Today Freed directs a staff of more than two hundred radio missionaries who broadcast in twenty-seven languages.

Similar circumstances propelled Dick Hillis to start Overseas Crusades, Inc. When World War II prevented Hillis and his family from returning to their mission station in China, he helped Hubert Mitchell, Dawson Trotman, and Bob Munger establish Los Angeles YFC. Each Saturday night Hillis gave a four-minute missionary challenge. In 1950 he headed a YFC team to Formosa where he witnessed thousands of new converts and heard Presbyterian missionary Dr. James Dickson say, "The church needs help in evangelism and in a training program for lay people." Hillis felt he should stay and "train each believer to use his occupation as his pulpit to make Christ known."

Dick Hillis still directs Overseas Crusades which now serves national churches in seven countries with literature, Bible correspondence courses (over 600,000 have enrolled), spiritual-life retreats, training of national evangelists, city-wide crusades, and traveling teams of "Bible-toting" basketball players under the Sports Ambassadors label.

Bob Finley, YFCI's second staff evangelist and before that a champion collegiate boxer and student-body president at the University of Virginia, received a different vision while evangelizing overseas. While in China Finley noticed that "nine out of ten of the revolutionary leaders had turned to Communism while studying abroad." Finley returned home and started the work now known as International Students, Inc. Instead of sending Americans abroad, ISI works among foreigners who are in the U.S. and Canada as students, diplomats, and tradesmen. Those who return home as Christian workers receive financial assistance by ISI for indigenous evangelism.

These missionary spin-offs each set a specialized ministry rolling. Numerous others moved into individual enterprises. Ken Anderson, pioneer producer of YFC films, left to start his own film production company. Ralph Carmichael, music director for Los Angeles YFC and several Winona conventions, went into big-time sacred and secular music production and recording. Russ Reid joined Word Records as vice-president and later set up his own advertising and publishing firm. These were only a few who had begun their ministry in YFC and then spun off into their own fields.

By 1955 so many of the old hands had left that Bob Cook wailed, "Everybody's bailing out except me."

However, he displayed confidence at Winona '56 that "the best is yet to come. We have more maturity, more humility, not so much grabbing for position and power," he said. "We are no longer a group of evangelical gadgeteers. The money situation is better. The statistics are thrilling—33,000 decisions in the rallies and 20,000 more in the clubs last year."

However, at an afternoon business session visiting speaker Bob Pierce dampened Bob Cook's enthusiasm. "You guys are trying to do too much," he said. "You aren't God's answer to every problem in the world. Do as we do in World Vision. Specialize in what you can do best—high school evangelism. God has other people to do the rest."

Pierce's blunt talk first shook, then challenged the staff. Men began saying, "He's right. We'd better start pruning the tree."

Seven months later, on Valentine's Day, 1957, Bob Cook resigned as YFCI president. Although he consented to step up to become chairman of the board, many felt he had deserted the ship.

The directors met in a lengthy emergency session and accepted Bob's choice, Ted Engstrom, to be acting president until the full convention of delegates met at Winona in July. Ted had been executive director since 1951 and, according to Bob, knew more about YFC than anybody else. He was loved as a Christian brother and respected as a good businessman, but many questioned if he was a strong enough personality to hold the organization together.

5

Guiding the Race Horses

Forty-one-year-old Ted Engstrom became the third president of YFCI. Although he was a big man, six-foot two, he was no arm-waving preacher like Torrey, nor was he a forceful charmer like Bob, nor did he have the Barrymore magnetism of Billy Graham. He could not even stride briskly to the platform because he limped from an old service injury incurred in a jeep accident. He looked like any teen's favorite uncle, and when he grinned his face squared into a warm glow. He was firm, reasonable Ted, a Christian and Missionary Alliance layman of unimpeachable integrity and an efficient executive who planned each day almost to the minute.

Ted Engstrom was more than just a Christian administrator, however. His concern for teenagers was genuine. Perhaps it stemmed from his high-school days when he was, in his own words, "the most miserable teenager in Cleveland, Ohio." It was a testimony which struck a familiar tune in the hearts of many high-school students. "My life was phony," he would say. "And I had my parents and everyone else thinking I was pretty good."

He managed to ward off all gospel influences until halfway through Taylor University. Then a charmer named Dorothy Weaver distressed him by turning down his requests for dates. The reason: "You're not a Christian, Ted." Those refusals started the process of events which led him to Jesus Christ and led Dorothy Weaver to become Mrs. Engstrom.

In 1957 Ted inherited the job of streamlining the octopus YFC organization. And when the delegates ratified his election at the Winona convention it seemed Ted had heeded Bob Pierce's advice.

First he spoke to the future: "If we double all of the work now being done for high schoolers in the next five years, we will barely have made a bit of progress toward reaching and winning this generation." Then he named the ministries to be emphasized: Saturday night rallies, high-school clubs, Lifeline, youth crusades, films, literature and summer camps and conferences.

Engstrom's leadership style was his own—and radically different from Torrey's direct commands or Cook's breezy directions (given with a dash of wit).

Ted sought a consensus. He would gather the staff together and hear them out, or he would fire off a batch of memos asking for comments on a topic. He gained a reputation as a notorious memo writer, and during one session in the hospital, the staff told inquirers he was having his memo gland removed. One Christmas they culled their files and presented him with a bound volume of hundreds of memos he had written.

Forever conscious of time and with an amazing capacity for work, Ted rarely squandered a minute. He would also chide his co-workers, "Wasted time is a sin that will face us in eternity. All of us were born lazy, so it takes determination and dedication to accomplish anything for Christ."

Serious internal problems faced the new president. Critics scrutinized every word of YFC's monthly magazine to be sure it was safe for kids to read. Bob Jones University, which had been advertising for ten years in the magazine, sent in an ad which YFC leaders considered unacceptable. The university refused to change the copy and has never advertised in the magazine since.

The Bob Jones quarrel (which actually centered on the criticism of Billy Graham by Dr. Bob Jones, Jr.) lost many supporters for YFC. Rally directors who sympathized with BJU continued their work but with little recognition of headquarters. Despite failing financial support, staff politics, disenchanted rally directors, YFC continued on a miracle basis. "God has taken YFC this far," Ted said frequently. "I believe He will keep it a continuing miracle."

The Lifeline program, for awhile under Wendy Collins, and then Bruce Love, touched the lives of teenagers in trouble, sometimes with amazing results. In Erie, Pennsylvania, YFC director Franklyn Miller visited a teenager who had just been sentenced to a state institution. George Irish was one of these kids who seemed destined for delinquency. "Something inside me," he once wrote, "kept turning me off the straight and narrow and into dangerous detours. I got through kindergarten okay, but from then on it was nothing but trouble."

Expelled from high school, he lived with a dream of being a crime boss. Finally, involvement in a stolen cigarette racket brought arrest. Out on bail, he and a friend burglarized a gas station. That was when the judge gave him a sentence of one to six years.

And that was when Miller gave him a copy of YFC magazine and a Billy Graham book. Miller and his friends prayed for Irish, now in jail, and at 6:00 P.M. on February 11, 1957, George became a Christian. He continued studying the Bible while in prison, memorizing hundreds of verses. Later he went to Philadelphia School of the Bible and is now a YFC director.

During the summer of 1960, 18 Lifeline camps in the U.S. and Canada welcomed problem boys—three years later the number had grown to 110. In Indiana, the State Youth Commission provided $10,000 to convert an old chicken farm into a Lifeline camp. Business firms provided food, play equipment, and other supplies, and more than twelve hundred troubled teenagers attended eleven one-week camps.

Campers came at the recommendation of probation officers, rally directors, and pastors, and college students served as counselors. A four-to-one camper-counselor ratio made possible the close relationships which kids, starved for adult friendship, desperately needed. Two-thirds of the campers that first summer professed to become Christians through the program.

And that fall, Indiana YFC men kept in contact with them through weekend retreats, parties, correspondence courses, and letter writing.

One of the teens at an Indiana camp one summer was Carden Henn. Henn had twelve sisters and nine brothers, all older than he. Home was impossible, with no chance of improvement, and

Lifeline boys then and Youth Guidance boys now find a strong masculine image in their counselor.

The YFC Youth Guidance program continues strong. Here, Doug Ross, former vice-president for the Northwest, counsels a boy in a Youth Guidance camp.

Below: Older teens browse through character-building books in a camp library.

YFC's
Capital
Teen Convention
drew 10,000 to
Washington, D.C.

Bill Eakin makes a grand entrance to the Portland, Oregon, rally.

Phil and Louie Palermo are a YFC institution. Here they are shown leading the singing in an early crusade. They currently serve as YFC International "special ambassadors," and recently sang and preached to U.S. servicemen in Vietnam.

he stole a car "so the authorities would have to take me away."

At camp Carden became a Christian. Soon he was at another YFC camp for further training. A counselor passing his cabin one day heard shouting and found a camper screaming to get out of a locked room.

"Carden did it," he cried.

"Yes," admitted the Lifeline boy. "I was talking to a boy in the bunk next to mine about the Lord and about the change in my life. But this kid kept interrupting and wouldn't let me talk. The only way I could get rid of him was to lock him in the room."

Back home Carden began to grow in Christ. He was placed in a foster home and at school raised his F average to B. Every time the lights went on at church he showed up. He even came to deacons' and Ladies' Aid meetings until someone explained.

Such successes encouraged YFCI to purchase the 101-acre farm in Fredericksburg, Virginia, where George Washington spent his boyhood. It was to be a youth home for needy boys. From plans for a $400,000 development program, a dormitory building was built and a museum started. However, expected support didn't materialize. Operating expenses and mortgage payments began draining the overall YFCI budget and the property had to be sold.

Club work continued to expand under Bill Eakin and reached an all-time high in 1960 with 2,763 clubs in the U.S., Canada, and overseas. Eakin, known as YFC's "court jester," passed on ideas through a column in *Eye*, a monthly dope sheet for YFC personnel. This, plus on-the-spot visits around the country by Eakin and other Wheaton staff members, and how-to sessions at Winona, kept club programs lively—and corny, by the standards of some outside critics.

One program suggestion called for a "Popcorn club meeting": Pop corn just before meeting so kids will smell and want to come. Hand each teen a bag of popcorn as he enters the room. Have "popcorn" testimonies. Introduce "Pop Korn" (dressed as old man) who will tell corny jokes and give announcements. Bring message that challenges kids to let God do for them what a little fire and oil can do for popcorn.

While critics groaned, Eakin and others slowly developed their own philosophy of teen evangelism. Eakin (pronounced *achin'*) wrote in his monthly column, "I really lose the victory when I go into a city or town and find a funspiration or party has been planned simply to give Christian teenagers a good time. We must major in this business of reaching teenagers with the gospel, by, (1) presenting a sharp teen-geared program that shows unsaved teens that Christians have a good time; (2) presenting the gospel in their own language and on their own level—short and to the point—and then giving them a chance to receive Christ."

In the same vein, YFC magazine editor Warren Wiersbe scolded YFC men for using the language of the church in the Saturday night rallies:

"YFC is not church, so why must we use church language? 'Brother Smith will now lead us in our opening prayer.' 'The YFC Choir is going to sing for us.' 'We're happy to have you in our service.' These phrases belong to the church; why bring them into a YFC rally?"

In most cities clubs still played second fiddle to the Saturday night rally, for which they were seen as feeders. Eakin said in 1960 what he wouldn't say later, "The mark of a good club program is its ability to make the Saturday night rally the key place in total YFC ministry."

But the rallies themselves had changed from the old days. Taking cues from show business, directors trained colored spotlights on program personalities, and on occasions presented gospel musicals à la Broadway. Detroit especially excelled in producing musicals with stage settings tastefully done to match the season.

The space age brought a new theme to YFC rally programming. Winona '58 set the pace by opening each evening's rally in the Billy Sunday Tabernacle with a blast-off. The teen chorus sounded the countdown, followed by the roll of drums, trumpet fanfare, and blast of rockets. Then Dr. Ted, as teens called him, read a Scripture portion and the chorus sang, "It Took a Miracle."

The old-time shouting, arm-waving, foot-stomping preachers from the early days became less and less popular. But not Don Lonie. With his dry wit and searing sentences, Lonie was geared to teens in the fifties. They understood what he meant when he said, "If Samson were living today, he'd lose his virtue in the back seat of a car at a drive-in."

Phil and Louie Palermo remained on the circuit, as well as converted professional entertainers like Tony Fontaine, Gloria Roe, and Bill Carle (the latter two were converted through YFC). Christian athletes like Bobby Richardson and Bob Davenport drew big crowds and delivered a straight Gospel. YFC directors exchanged podiums and used men from the headquarters staff. Films could be booked from several organizations, since YFC had earlier showed conservative Christians that the movie camera could glorify God. With such an abundance of proven communicators the old-time preachers scarcely had a chance.

Requests kept coming to headquarters asking for help in getting new YFC rallies started. Often the petitioners were teenagers who were turned on at Winona and couldn't wait to spread the enthusiasm back home. In the old days a field man would have been sent to organize a board and rent an auditorium. But many rallies had collapsed because of lack of interest, unpaid bills, and, in a few situations, scandals. Ted Engstrom knew that more had to be done, and set up a "Target City" program.

The pattern was the same in each city. Special funds were raised, then a veteran director moved in to lead know-how seminars for teens and adults already interested. He talked to the people essential to the success of a new program—pastors, school administrators, and Christian businessmen. He set up a temporary committee, started clubs, found a good Saturday night rallying place, then scheduled "proven communicators" for future rallies. Miami in '59 and Houston in '61 took root and developed into strong rallies. Salt Lake City fizzled out, probably because of its small evangelical constituency.

Overseas, Sam Wolgemuth was quietly logging thousands of air miles, planting the seeds of YFC work in South America, Africa, Europe, the Far East. Missionaries in dozens of countries got to know him, respected him, and extended their ministry to youth at his urging.

Sam had long felt the urgency for nationals to take over control of YFC work from the missionaries. But the visa problem he encountered in getting Americans to the Eighth World Congress of Evangelism in Madras, India, convinced him and other YFCI leaders that there was less time left than they had imagined.

Sam had applied for forty visas four months in advance. But trouble came because of a fund-raising pamphlet (intended for the U.S. audience only) which suggested that time for evangelism was running out in India because of the Communist threat. The visas were denied less than a week before scheduled departure, apparently because Indian officials had read and seen political implications in the pamphlet.

Sam phoned cooperating missionary Cliff Robinson in New Delhi. Robinson asked for a cable stating that YFCI was a nonpolitical religious organization to present to Premier Nehru, the only one who could reverse the denials. Sam sent the cable and waited in New York while the others flew on to Beirut, Lebanon, anticipating action by Nehru. In an amazing sequence of events that Sam cites as a miracle, Robinson got the cable to Nehru and the prime minister acted favorably.

In some places national roots took hold and grew. In others YFC workers continually touched young hearts but saw no program develop. At the close of World Vision's Tokyo Crusade, where Wolgemuth and others represented Youth for Christ, Sam sent back reports of youth meetings.

A student at Yasuda-Gakuen, an engineering school in Tokyo, had arranged for youth workers to visit his school. More than a hundred male students pushed into a small classroom wondering what it was all about. A gospel team sang and gave testimonies, then Sam, who was no newcomer to Japan, preached the gospel. He dismissed the meeting with an invitation to those who wanted to receive Christ as Saviour to stay behind.

Seventy-eight remained.

"Now," Sam wrote, "just as clearly as I knew how, I explained that Christ had died for the sins of the world, that trusting Him would make them God's children and give them eternal life; that they could be saved from sin right there."

Fifty-three made decisions to receive Christ.

The fifties were fading quickly and YFCI, now in its teen years, was anxious to stay geared to the times. From the postwar patriotic rallies they had moved, along with one-third of the nation, into suburbia. YFC was growing up. Now, fascinated with the future, as most Americans were, and impressed by the sheer rapidity of change, YFC leaders dubbed the coming sixties "The Decade of Destiny."

On this platform they launched a Capital Teen Convention the week before New Year's Day, 1960. Ten thousand teenagers rode the bus, flew, took the train, or drove into Washington, D.C., creating a staggering housing and feeding problem. Hotel managers, usually fearful of holiday high-school crowds, gaped in surprise at their guests' orderly behavior. One boy brought a ripped pillow case to a manager and offered to pay for it. The hotel man shook his head in disbelief, remembering senior classes that had left curtains in shreds.

On the White House lawn where delegates took part in the lighting of the national Christmas tree, President Eisenhower commended the teenagers and YFC leaders.

Not all of the delegates in Washington were committed Christian youth. Many came to spend a holiday in the capital, but hundreds walked to the front of the National Armory at the invitation of Billy Graham and other evangelists to accept Christ.

In Denver, on the eve of the Capital Teen Convention registration deadline, a Sunday school teacher put up the money for one of his students to go. Paul Phillips was not a model teen. In fact, he and his gang "the Northside 44thers" were on a year's probation, charged with gang warfare, using chains, lead pipes, hammers, and so on to fight.

At one of the convention meetings the gospel got through to Paul. He knew he was a new person when he walked out of the inquiry room. Back in Denver the real test came. He was failing every subject in school and the semester would end in three weeks. Paul worked, crammed, prayed, made up all his homework and passed each course. By the end of the next semester he had a B average as well as having dropped out of the gang and having moved into church and YFC activities.

A second Capital Teen Convention in December, 1962, drew another ten thousand teens. Several weeks after that, YFC leaders meeting at a midwinter convention in Denver found themselves faced with Ted Engstrom's resignation.

It wasn't unexpected. His old leg injury was even more painful after an unsuccessful operation. One day he told a YFC group, "You men are like a bunch of race horses. I can't stay up with you. I can only try and keep your noses pointed in the right direction."

His resignation turned the convention into more of a political caucus than a gathering of youth workers. Factions gathered in hotel rooms to plot strategy for favorite personalities. West Coasters wanted a president from their ranks. Men from the East felt their area deserved the honor. Some wanted a man who would bring back the conservative defectors and others looked ahead to more fellowship with mainline denominational churches. "Too many acted like second-class ward politicians," a YFC leader recalls today.

Finally after two days of wrangling, they elected a compromise candidate. Carl "Kelly" Bihl had been a rally director, a field evangelist, and most recently the director of leadership development. Kelly had spoken at just about everybody's rally. He was known as a "good preacher" and "a man of prayer," though his administrative talents were unproven.

6

Voyage Into A New Era

In 1963, YFC's nineteen-year-old slogan—"Geared to the Times and Anchored to the Rock"—was becoming increasingly difficult to follow. Staying anchored to the Rock wasn't the problem, but in an age where change grew upon change at computerized speed, keeping geared to the times demanded daily updating of both information and methodology.

This was the age of technology, the electronic age, the TV age, the space age. It was also the day in which Americans, always a people in motion, were on the move even more. Great population shifts marked the sixties. Millions now worked in the suffering cities but lived in the suburbs. No one was left to pay taxes, slums grew, crime increased.

That vast wasteland of culture, TV, stole a thousand or more hours a year from teenagers. It also made them more knowledgeable than any previous generation, and, according to many educators and sociologists, resulted in fantasy living, poor study habits, alienation, and a pattern of thinking foreign to book-educated adults.

The sixties saw the beginning of a credit-buying craze and increased government control to restrain advertising, prices, wages, credit, and so on. The paperback book revolution continued. Newspaper and magazine circulation grew but the number of them declined. Church attendance began to wane. Tourism increased.

For two of those years, Kelly Bihl, as the fourth president of

YFCI, rode a stormy sea of dissatisfaction. He presided over an exodus of older directors and arbitrated a struggle for credentialing men (qualifying them for regular staff) and raising rally standards. The conflicts tore deep into the organization and into the heart of a man whose main gift and experience to that time had been preaching and teaching the Word of God.

Before becoming president, Kelly's usual solution to problems was, "Let's pray." When, after a first round of prayers the problem was still up in the air, he would say, "Let's pray some more." And sometimes after praying the moon to bed, men would start confessing wrong attitudes, admitting mistakes, and agreeing to work in harmony.

Now he saw that more than prayer was needed to pilot the ship through the stormy waters of opinion. Problems pressed; solutions were slow in coming. In March, 1965, Kelly resigned to join the radio staff of John Brown University.

In those two years, perhaps the most tumultuous in YFC's twenty, he served as a respected spiritual leader. And he bore bruises as a buffer during a period when YFC was narrowing its ministry and as a result losing men whose talents and interests were not solely in high school evangelism.

The delegates to the January, 1965, Midwinter Convention unanimously elected a Pennsylvania farmer's son as the fifth president of YFCI. Sam Wolgemuth, a bishop in his small Brethren in Christ denomination, for nine years the director of YFCI Overseas Ministries, a quiet self-assured minister of the gospel as well as successful businessman, took up the task which had severely shaken the emotional and physical fortitude of several fine men before him.

Ten years of overseas travel had given Wolgemuth a world awareness far beyond that of his days as a pastor in Franklin County. There, as a prewar Taylor University graduate, he had taken a job selling farm implements to supplement the twenty dollars a month which his church offered him. Evenings and weekends he moved among the plain people of his church, ministering to their spiritual needs. In the daytime he met with farmers, talked them into up-to-date agricultural tools. Both the business and the parish prospered and Sam felt the need of work which kept him closer to home. He considered buying a hardware business.

In a local auto parts store one morning he made his third inquiry in as many hours about a water pump the parts man was rebuilding for him. It still hadn't been touched and Sam in frustration protested, "Mrs. Stouffer, if you can't run the business, why don't you sell it?"

"Mr. Wolgemuth," she replied, "we'd gladly sell it if we could find a buyer."

That evening Sam quietly told his wife, Grace, they were to be the new owners of an auto parts store.

Not until the summer of 1949 did the course of YFC collide with the life of the Pennsylvania pastor. Sam attended a summer refresher course at the seminary at Winona Lake, Indiana, that year. While he studied Grace wandered down the hill to the conference grounds to find a YFCI convention in progress.

The spectacle was like nothing she had encountered before. She was awed and touched and sure that God was in the midst of the enthusiasm she witnessed.

Deeply moved, she hurried up the hill, and only with some urging could she tear her diligent husband from the books. That summer night, as Sam and Grace sat halfway back in the Billy Sunday Tabernacle, God spoke to them about something they sensed in the lives of the men around them and something they wanted in their own lives.

The convention closed before the Wolgemuths made real contact with the YFC leaders. Sam continued his course and the Bible conference went on with Lutheran radio pastor Walter B. Maier as the speaker. This time Sam did speak to the conference leaders. He shared his conviction with Maier that God was calling him to step out and do something. Maier asked him if he had given everything he had to his church. "No," Sam confessed, and the older man counseled, "Go back and give them everything you have."

His first Sunday back in Waynesboro, Sam stood in the pulpit and told his people he hadn't done his best for them. Men in the congregation were moved and likewise confessed their lack of support for the pastor. God met with His people in that church, and the next year was a rich one of blessing for the little congregation. A year later Sam and Grace returned to Winona and God spoke to them again—this time very clearly about leaving the church for a ministry in YFC.

The final step came months later when Bob Pierce, now a good friend of the Wolgemuths, came to Waynesboro for a World Vision rally. Pierce urged Sam to move his family to Japan to set up YFC's World Congress there the next year. In the Wolgemuth's home that night he called Bob Cook in Chicago and announced before a startled Grace, "I have your man for Japan."

Now it was Grace's turn to balk. She resented Pierce's "high-handed" way and off-handedly told him, "It will be a miracle if I ever get peace about going to Japan."

Days later, in a meeting in which a friend was speaking, God reminded her that "He never takes anything out of our lives without giving us something better in return." This was what she needed to give her peace to leave the Waynesboro congregation. Months after that they were on the boat heading for Japan.

In the thirteen intervening years before he became president, the inevitable white specked Sam's temples, his natural reserve developed into dignity, and the auto parts business multiplied into a four-store chain. The new president was more like Ted Engstrom than any of his predecessors. He was an organization man, a careful planner who invited confidences by the way he listened. He had the capacity to feel deeply, then act wisely after hearing out his colleagues on an important issue.

Above all, Sam was flexible and open to change. Directors admired him because he related to his three teenagers at home. He moved easily in a McLuhan age, while standing firmly on the Biblical fundamentals YFC had always proclaimed.

Sam showed no desire to become an evangelical Dean Martin or a YFC version of Pat Boone. He chose not to author a teen advice column in the magazine as past presidents had done. By nature he simply didn't have the razzmatazz to become the honoree of a teen fan club. Grace matched him in quiet dignity, wore longer dresses than other YFC wives and sometimes wore her hair in a bun.

But Sam Wolgemuth was the man of the hour for an organization that had long struggled to become a cohesive team. "The Bishop" moved quickly to assume leadership of the five division heads in the headquarters office: Bill Eakin, Campus Life (clubs); Wendy Collins, Overseas Ministries (he moved up when Sam became president); Bruce Love, Lifeline; Harold Myra, Literature (also the magazine editor); and Jay Kesler, Leadership Development. To these five, Sam quickly added a sixth cabinet member, layman Paul Van Oss, to be executive director.

Paul Van Oss had had little contact with YFC before. He was a Wheaton College graduate who had turned a good profit in a hardware manufacturing company in Minneapolis. But God had spoken to him—before Sam did—and he had sold his partnership in the business and invested in a restaurant franchise that gave him financial support but demanded little of his time. Then with a conviction that some Christian organization needed the business know-how and experience God had given him, Paul waited for direction from God.

The direction came through Sam Wolgemuth and on April 1, 1965, PVO, as he was soon titled, moved into the Wheaton headquarters.

It wasn't that easy, however, to move into control and apply his organizational strategy, as he called it, to YFC. His initiation to the ministry and the men was colorful. The first night he joined YFC was for a board meeting in Denver. About twenty-five directors and veeps had gathered and before the meeting split into two groups for dinner. One group escorted Paul to a restaurant and vigorously sang "Happy Birthday" to him. It wasn't his birthday. At the end of the meal they presented him with a gift—the bill for the food they had just eaten. Then, in high humor, they proceeded to the meeting, nearly an hour late, and solemnly declared to Sam it was all Paul's fault.

Paul survived the initiation in good spirits and quickly exhibited a creativity in business areas that surprised many. With typical Dutch determination he tackled the persistent financial problems, outlined long-range business goals and filled in the steps to achieve them.

With an eye for more efficiency, Van Oss rented IBM 360 data processing equipment to increase the direct mail program for fund raising. When someone suggested YFC might lose the miracle touch to a computer, Paul, unsmiling, replied, "God has given us tools like the computer. We'll do all in our power and then turn to God for the miracle touch. God doesn't expect us to sit back and wait for things to fall in our laps."

At the same time Paul began to accomplish something within the organization, his personal life took on a new meaning. "I had felt for a while a gnawing dissatisfaction," he told the men, "that I wasn't living at full potential. Now I'm completely relaxed in that area, knowing that I'm accomplishing something not merely for a day, but in the lives of young people."

Sam's man in charge of developing leadership, Jay Kesler, had come from a different family mold than the average YFC man. The son of a politically liberal, non-church-going labor leader in South Bend, Indiana, young Jay had felt church simply irrelevant to his socially successful high-school life. He did well in class also, was a student body officer and was involved in county-wide politics.

A few weeks before school closed in his junior year in high school, he heard singing one day from a classroom. It was a YFC club, and Kesler decided the most interesting thing he could do at the moment was to disturb the peace.

The sight of a class officer, top student, and social swinger walking in the door so shocked the YFC clubbers they stopped singing in the middle of their song. Nervously they regained their composure and began another. Then a fellow stood and talked about what Christ had done in his life. When the group bowed their heads to pray, Jay, embarrassed and troubled, got up and walked out.

Next day in the lunchroom a group of the YFC kids sat near Jay. When they bowed their heads to pray before eating, they drew an irreverent comment from a nearby teacher. That in turn drew Kesler to the Christians' defense.

Surprising himself, he commented, "It seems to me that if they're going to believe this stuff they should believe it all the time, not just on Sunday."

Later in the day he ran across Phyllis, one of the YFC club leaders, who asked him, "Didn't I see you in our YFC meeting yesterday?"

"Yes," he reluctantly admitted.

"Well," she pinned him, "What did you think of it?"

He answered honestly, "I didn't think it was fair of you to talk about me the way you did in front of all those kids."

"We weren't talking about you," she smiled. "For *all* have sinned and come short of the glory of God," and she went on to explain the gospel to him.

Suddenly it was clear to him. Phyllis persisted. "Is there any reason why you can't let Christ into your life right now?"

Jay looked around. They were standing in the school corridor. "Well," he hesitated, "this is sort of a private thing. I don't think you can do it here in the hall."

Not to be put off, Phyllis led him to a curtained-off spot behind the stage in the school auditorium. There she taught him phrase for phrase how to pray, to seek forgiveness, and to ask Jesus Christ to control his life.

Shortly after that the new Christian found that a group of YFC teens had gathered before school each day in the library to pray specifically for him.

Later, as a psychology major at Taylor University, Jay directed a nearby YFC program. After graduation he served as a regional director for Illinois and Indiana, then joined the headquarters staff as Kelly Bihl's assistant for leadership development.

The young recruiter liked John F. Kennedy, whereas YFC's conservative constituency had been, according to one jokester, "the Republican Party at prayer." He felt that American evangelicalism was too wedded to conservative, middle-class society; too business-oriented, with very little ministry to the laboring man; too much an unbalanced subculture that had cut itself off from gut issues of the times. Thus he appealed to young men who themselves were reacting to religious institutions that had retreated from the mainstream of modern living.

Kesler found many eager to serve with YFC but lacking in know-how. He encouraged colleges to offer special courses in youth ministries with credit for both classroom instruction and on-the-job training as assistants to YFC personnel in the area. Bethel College, Trinity Evangelical Divinity School, Fuller Theological Seminary, and Seattle Pacific College agreed to do so.

Graduates who lacked experience were offered a year's internship under experienced men, after which they could apply for credentials or move to another Christian organization.

Kesler and a few other YFC men (notably Jack Daniel in

Chicago) began a program to develop black leadership. Daniel, a long-time YFC veteran, wanted black men to direct clubs in predominantly black Chicago high schools.

Bill Pannell, an articulate young black minister from Detroit who came in as associate director of Leadership Training, soon found he had a saddle but no horse. Very few black young people were attending evangelical colleges, and the few prospects he found were hesitant to join a "lily-white" organization. Some blacks hinted that Pannell himself was a "Tom." After three years he reluctantly resigned, feeling he could better witness to his people by working with other black men. "The problem is one of time differential," he said. "Ten years ago you could have recruited young blacks when they were pushing for integration. But their mood has now changed."

The concern for blacks spilled over into the magazine, which had previously skirted the civil rights issue. Not until 1964, under Ron Wilson, did the magazine begin talking about civil rights and prejudice and showing pictures of attractive black teens.

Under Harold Myra the magazine became contemporary in other ways. It got a new name, *Campus Life,* plus splashy colors. Harold and his associate Dean Merrill, a 6′7″ former teen teamer, began warming the pages with provocative articles geared to the swinging sixties that would have singed the hair of early YFC men.

Early in his editorship Myra printed a letter from a hippie-type radical and titled it "Beards, Sandals, and Socialism—a youthful Marx-eye view of American Christianity." "No longer do your holy churches get their WASP hands dirty," the angry student wrote. "Praise the Lord and pass the money. Let's be happy and nice and step where it helps, not hurt. Hey, don't Christians carry crosses anymore?" Myra's printed comment: "He typifies a criticism of the Christian's noninvolvement in social issues . . . which cannot be ignored."

Such articles splattered beside breezy photos of stylishly dressed black and white kids mixed together brought worried letters from some skittish YFC directors saying in effect, "The articles are great for the kids but are hurting my fund raising."

The magazine itself reflected in many ways an emerging club

philosophy and program and the mind of the man behind it—Bill Eakin. For six years Eakin had barnstormed, spent more time on the road than at home, lived every possible minute with teenagers and directors and collected a file and head full of ideas.

A typical trip carried him into the West Coast on the late late flight, arriving at 1:30 A.M. He grabbed a few hours in a motel and was up at 5:30 A.M. for exercises. At 6:15 A.M. he ate breakfast with the local director and at 7:00 A.M. met with forty students in the music room of a suburban high school. The director then rushed him out to get downtown to Central High by 7:40 A.M. One hour later with the city's teenagers in class, Bill talked about them to the local YFC board.

At 12:15 P.M. he stood before sixty teens in a living room a block off campus, and a half hour later forty junior highers took the older teens' place. After school it was another club; then at 6:45 P.M. twenty-four college students, part-time YFC club workers, sat in the director's living room for a know-how session.

The evening meeting was in the school auditorium, and counseling after that carried on for an hour until the nervous director dragged him away to the airport. At 11:15 P.M. he was airborne again, heading for the next city.

Gradually his philosophy of youth work sharpened. Bill was in touch with the grass roots and in a position to see and select the best. "The era of the pat answer is gone," he preached to adults. "You can't just give a kid a certain verse, tell him to pray, pat him on the head, and send him away with his problem. He'll fall on his nose again and again. We've got to help the kid understand himself, his problems, and his environment, and show him the principles that, when applied, can put his life in balance."

Bill and a half dozen of the nation's top youth workers developed a philosophy they called the balanced life. Eakin himself tried to live it. And he built a reputation over the years for a genuine concern for teenagers that regularly brought him to tears.

Wendy Collins recalls the first time he met Bill at a summer camp. Wendy was the speaker and Bill was doing know-how sessions and counseling. "Late the first night, I came back to the cabin to find Bill on his knees, sobbing into one of the old bunk beds. No one had accepted the Lord that night and he was broken. Later that night teenagers, one by one, came to the cabin to seek him out and accept Jesus Christ as Saviour."

Eakin picked up the title "Pied Piper of Teens." He was an instant success with teens individually or in groups in any country. Quick to detect insincerity, teenagers sensed that his interest in them was genuine. Two who met Eakin at YFC camps in Ohio and New York one hot August were typical.

A friend had paid the way for a sixteen-year-old named Jay to attend camp. Antagonistic and rebellious, he began tearing the camp apart—and his big athletic build helped. Bill got to know Jay and with their interest in sports they found common ground. When Jay finally took Christ as his Saviour, he did a complete turnabout. "It reminded me of the switch in the Apostle Paul's life," Bill wrote. "He turned from negative to positive."

Judy was a cheerleader, an All-American type from a Roman Catholic background, with not much previous contact with YFC. The first night that Bill gave an invitation for teenagers to receive Christ, she decided that was what she needed. That was Sunday. On Tuesday she found Eakin and told him, "I want to get involved. On Sunday night God got one foot in the door of my life. Now I want Him to get in with both." Bill talked with her and later heard her pray, "Lord, come into every room in my house."

The balanced life philosophy the YFC men developed was built on a verse in Luke (2:52), the only Biblical reference to Christ's days as a teenager. "And Jesus increased in wisdom," said to these men that Christ developed a mental dimension in His life. The reference to "stature" was, of course, his physical growth. "And in favor with God" they interpreted as a spiritual dimension, and finally, the words "in favor with . . . man" told them Christ had a social side to His life.

They stuck the tag "The Balanced Life" on the concept and came up with an official description: "The Balanced Life is the philosophy that strives to develop a spiritual, physical, mental, and social balance in the life of the Christian teenager that will enable him to properly and successfully communicate in action and word his personal faith in Jesus Christ to his friends, his campus and his world."

From this base, YFC men began working at meeting the needs

of high school students who, with the old approach, were not developing sufficient maturity or effectiveness as Christians. As a result of much experimentation, the "Insight/Impact" concept evolved. One week the meeting would be called Impact and would be geared especially for non-Christian kids. Insight would meet the next week and train Christian teens.

The men on the field with the best ideas and concepts fed their materials through headquarters, which gave them professional polish and distributed them nationally.

The concept revolutionized the club program and eventually moved Eakin out of the Wheaton office. He saw his country-wide barnstorming as part of the past. With an eye to the special problems of the big city, Eakin moved to Long Island to direct an urban program, with a direct tie to the Wheaton office.

Under Gary Dausey, who had been working with Jay Kesler at headquarters, a totally new training ministry was launched. Adult "Seminars on Teen Dynamics" were sponsored by YFC and local church associations, and YFC men shared their expertise with pastors, Christian education directors, Sunday school teachers and parents. Often they called in local experts such as sociology or Christian-education professors.

Forty such institutes were held in two years, involving nine thousand adults from all major denominations. In Milwaukee and Charlotte, Catholic teaching nuns attended. Some later ordered YFC program materials and reported girls who had "trusted in Christ."

After an institute, one church in Denver began a Sunday morning class for parents of younger children "to prevent some of the teen problems revealed at the Institute." They also compiled a list of teenagers to pray for daily.

More success came from a new thrust overseas, patterned after the Peace Corps. The "Y-2" program sent qualified college graduates abroad for two years to work under national YFC leadership. Bill and Ellen Spade were the first couple to go in 1966. Bill, an Indiana music graduate, had met Ellen, a Norwegian, while on a '62 Teen Team trip to Scandinavia. The Spades went to Norway where Bill earned partial support by teaching music and art in a Norwegian Lutheran church school. They organized an international youth choir that sang on tele-

Rosemary Nachtigal
of California
cut a folk record with WORD,
sang in rallies, and
travelled on a '69 Teen Team.

vision and made several tours singing and giving testimonies in Norwegian state churches. The youth choir ministry opened doors for the Spades to organize the first YFC clubs in Norwegian schools.

The new Teen Team program expanded (see chapter 9) and individual Americans, studying or working overseas, carried on corners of youth evangelism for YFC. In one instance Dave Pilcher, a high school graduate from Elgin, Illinois, spent a year in West Berlin with American director Bill Yoder, preparing for the Teen Team coming the next year. Pilcher lived in a fifth-floor, cold-water room in a bombed-out building. "It was almost comical," he wrote home, "taller than it was wide. I used to lie in bed at night thinking how much more room I'd have if I could lay it on its side."

In another case a teenager from Utica, Michigan, spent a

summer assisting Peruvian YFC workers. Nanci Goodwine told her own story:

"For eight weeks I visited high schools and clubs, sang, talked to students, answered a thousand questions about the U.S., my boyfriend, my school, and told my Peruvian friends about Jesus Christ. High in the Andes I trudged the dusty streets of small towns selling Bibles and Christian books to stone-faced Indians, trying in my broken Spanish to tell them they could have the Word of God."

At the end of the summer she and YFC workers took sixteen North American teenagers deep into Shipibo Indian country to a mission station which only Jungle Aviation and Radio Service could get them into. Eight of the campers were Christians; eight were not. Between alligator hunts, invasions of army ants, jungle hikes, canoe trips and the like, they presented Jesus Christ and the Christian life to the teens.

On the last night of camp one of the resident missionaries spoke to the group. Nanci described it: "I must have prayed through most of the meeting because before I knew it, Dave was making a strange request of everyone.

" 'Take off your right shoe,' he commanded. 'Put it in this box.'

"Then to the sixteen waiting campers he threw his challenge. 'Your life is something like this shoe . . . a little worn, perhaps, dirty in spots. Some of these shoes have been places they shouldn't have been. Now what will you do with your life? Turn it over to God? Or discard it like an old shoe? You've heard the claims of Jesus Christ. What are you going to do with Him?'

"Slowly he picked up each shoe, held it up for its owner to claim it and returned it with the question, 'What will you do with Jesus Christ tonight? Don't answer to me. Answer to God. Think about it.'

"Through tears I watched each teenager silently take his own shoe from Dave. I took mine and put it on the floor, unable to put it on as I thought of the day in which I met Jesus Christ as my Saviour. Again I prayed for each of them.

"Yes, I prayed. Fully expecting God to answer? That's a tough question, but I do know that when Dave invited them to make decisions for Jesus Christ then and there, and all but one stood up, it was clearly beyond my expectations. All I could do was thank the Lord—over and over again—for the teenagers who had turned over their lives to Jesus Christ and for the privilege of watching God work in my life and in theirs."

One of Sam Wolgemuth's dreams when he was overseas director was a world congress in Jerusalem for teenagers. He had the encouragement of Israeli officials and had stirred up interest in YFC directors on several continents. When the North American delegates killed the idea in 1962, a backlash of criticism came from overseas men. It pointed up what Sam had struggled with for several years and what many missionary groups had known for much longer—national Christian groups which have sprung from an American movement expect full recognition as national bodies, not as junior partners. The time had come to pull YFC together in a truly international body.

The year before he became president, Sam and YFC men from around the world met in Switzerland and outlined an international council. They met again in 1966; then in 1968 they put together a constitution and bylaws, and the North American organization, which had claimed the international title for so long, became one more equal partner in a world-wide council. New Zealander Ray Harrison, a former salesman with a chemical firm and for years YFC director in several spots in Asia, was elected executive secretary and a year later set up an international office in Geneva, Switzerland.

In January, 1969, Sam Wolgemuth was unanimously re-elected president for the fifth straight year. The enthusiasm with which the delegates voted for him bespoke a belief that the years of internal turmoil were behind and years of unparalleled opportunity for youth evangelism were ahead.

PART II

YOUTH FOR CHRIST TODAY

7

Shock It to Me

The portable sign stuck in the snow says: CAMPUS LIFE MEETS HERE 7:30. You check your watch as a big jet swooshes over the rooftop for a landing at nearby O'Hare Airport. A redheaded housewife opens the door and looks puzzled. You're over thirty. She points to the stairs and smiles. "Sit here. If you feel like you're in the way, you probably are."

Wall-to-wall teenagers. Gary DeClute, the Campus Life director, is in turtleneck sweater and slacks, and he has long sideburns. "C'mon, stuff in real tight, gang. Make room for the latecomers," he says.

You try to count the heads and give up. There must be at least a hundred and fifty senior high kids sitting in the living and dining rooms.

"Hurreee up, gang. Pass out the ballpoints and paper. You on this side write the *bys*. You over here write the *hows*. We've done it before. You know how it's done.

"Okay, now pass 'em up to the guy and gal at the front. Move it! Move it! We've only got an hour."

He points to the boy in the brown cardigan and the brunette in the green mini-skirt. The boy reads, "How do you pick up a girl?" The girl reads, "By polishing your toe nails."

Peals of laughter.

"How do you water ski through chocolate ice cream?"

"By smoking asparagus."

"How do you make beer?"

"By taking a bath."

"How do you control an impulse?"

"By taking it off."

A few more how's and by's, and then, "Okay, gang, I need ten beautiful girls. C'mon."

Ten girls are pushed to the front. Gary hands each a balloon. "Blow 'em until they pop. Last one to pop gets the chair."

The girls puff. The audience yells. Bang! Bang! Bang! Now only the little blonde remains.

Gary pushes forward an odd-looking stool with a battery underneath and holds a black cord that runs to the chair. With his thumb on a small switch, he cackles, "Have a seat, Jeri."

The little blonde eases onto the chair, face set, fists clenched. "We always give the chair to people who have problems. Ready for the countdown—ten, nine, eight . . ." The kids count with him. He pushes the switch. The blonde squeals at being jolted, giggles, and goes back to her place.

"Now who brought dates?" A dozen or so hands go up. "Fine, I need three couples to come up. The gals will go first while you guys go in the other room."

"Okay, Pat, you're first. Three questions: Where did you go on your first date? Was your boy friend generous, average, or tight in spending money? Did he kiss you on your first date?"

Pat answers each question, then he asks the other two girls.

The boys are brought in and one by one are asked the same questions. The first one who answers differently from his date gets the chair. "Yeoow!" Same with the second and third. They get the chair, too. Howls of laughter each time from the crowd.

Twenty minutes have passed.

Five minutes for announcements. Gary tells about a coming big event and points out two kids. "Get your ticket from them right away or you'll be left out. We can only take two hundred."

"Okay, let's have a little talk about a pretty popular subject which affects all of us right where we live—sex."

Knowing looks appear on the kids' faces.

"Some parents asked me a while back what's the difference between high-school kids today and those of the past. I told them I thought today's kids are more honest and open. That's why I always look forward to a discussion on a subject like this, because it calls for each of us to express himself honestly.

"Now for about twenty-five minutes we're going to talk about sex and morality. We have two guidelines for the discussion: First, only one person speaks at a time, and second, you give a person a chance to finish before you agree or disagree with him.

"Okay, ready for the first question: Who sets the standard on a date—the guy, the girl, or her mother?"

A few seconds of awkward silence. "Well," Gary drawls satirically, "I didn't know sex and dating was such a burning issue around Elk Grove." Kids laugh.

A husky boy in a letterman's jacket, "The girl. She has ways of telling a guy how far he can go."

Another boy, "I agree. No guy is going to try and make out with a girl who holds her standards up."

More discussion, then another question, "What determines how far you go on a date?"

Still another boy, "Where you are, man. I mean, like a drive-in is different from a bowling alley."

Now a girl, "I don't agree. It's what you are. A girl doesn't have to give in to a boy at a drive-in."

More discussion, then the final question: "Okay, let's have some opinions on whether you think premarital sex is right or wrong."

Boy: "I don't think you can answer that question with a strict yes or no. Sometimes it is. Sometimes it isn't. It depends on what you think about the girl."

Girl: "An answer like that makes me boil. You think some girls are things just to satisfy your animal appetite. I'm people and sex is a very important, uh, personal thing with me." She blushes and sits down.

Heated discussion. Some take the position premarital sex is okay between consenters and if the girl is on the pill. Some say it's okay if the boy and girl are in love. Some say that sex is most meaningful only in marriage.

Gary breaks in. "Our discussion time is up. I've listened to your comments because I respect them. Now, would you listen to me for about five minutes?

"Too many guys and girls live for just two things: their stomachs and their glands! They know a lot about the plumbing, but not much about the meaning. The mistake they make is they don't know the difference between two four-letter words: love and lust."

He defines the words and then quotes Ann Landers' answer to a girl whose boy friend is saying, "How will you know how it feels if you never try it?" "Ann Landers wrote back, 'Tell him to go and stick his head in a cement mixer—how does he know how it will feel—he's never tried that before, either!' "

When the laughing dies down Gary defines the Playboy philosophy, then zeroes in on "God's purpose for sex—a unique human experience to be shared in the fullest love, in marriage."

His voice falls. He leans towards the kids who are astoundingly quiet. "I'm not saying I'm a superman who finds it easy to withstand the same temptations and pressures that you have. But I've found a tremendous power that helps me face these problems and keep myself for the girl I intend to marry."

He talks about God's power to overcome sexual pressures, then God's willingness to forgive those "who have already made mistakes."

And finally, "If you'd like to have this power in your life, and His forgiveness, I'll be glad to talk to you. There's a stack of appointment cards with pencils in the kitchen. Put your name on one and I'll get in touch with you."

The mob rises and struggles toward the kitchen where the hostess has piled eleven half-gallon blocks of ice cream into a tub. She passes around three cans of chocolate syrup and three cans of whipped cream. The kids make the "world's biggest sundae," then help themselves.

Half an hour later they are gone. Gary picks up five cards with names. Tomorrow he will follow them up for counsel. Two or three probably will start coming to his much smaller Insight group which meets the following week.

Such is a Campus Life Impact club meeting. The crowdbreakers vary; at the next meeting, Gary may use the pie machine which works like Russian roulette and plasters one kid out of six taking a chance. Or the lie detector. Or the time bomb. Or the chair again, also known as the original Bunsen burner and the shock-it-to-me chair. He will certainly lead an open discussion on a topic of teen interest and at least half of the kids present will be non-Christians. In the non-churchy atmosphere, away from adults, they will feel free to speak honestly and some will later confide in Gary.

Every Impact and Insight meeting is programed, and planned manuals explain how to use the crowdbreakers and the discussions to confront teenagers with Christ in an informal, casual atmosphere.

The electric chair is the most-used piece of crowdbreaking equipment. Just about every YFC group has one or more, and no man's training is complete until he knows how to use the brain-child of Ken Overstreet in San Diego.

Overstreet, a slim, personable 31-year-old, recently elected member of the San Diego Board of Education, defends its use to disturbed adults. "The shock from the small six-volt battery is jolting but harmless. It isn't sadistic."

The chairs and other fun devices are also part of the new geared-to-the-times look in YFC Saturday Nites—the title now preferred by some instead of rallies. Modern YFC Saturday Nites must compete with a variety of fun things. Long Beach, California, YFC, for example, must make itself a better drawing card than Disneyland, Melodyland, Marineland, big-time sports, and other tantalizers only minutes along the freeway.

Long Beach's Don Goehner honeys them into a supper club atmosphere where the format, dress, and staging are casual. The music—sacred and secular—is folk, sometimes a little rock, with the sacred usually in a folk setting. Don will interview a key high-school student, not necessarily a Christian, and program a takeoff on Laugh-In, Mission Impossible, or some other well-known show.

A recent Mission Impossible sent three boys out with squirt guns with instructions to trade up to the most valuable item they could find within a specified time limit. One brought back a $400 trumpet, another a $10 bottle of perfume, and another talked a guy into driving his convertible in front of the rally.

Near the end they bring on a teen communicator. After the speaker finishes Don invites teens interested in knowing more to stay for a talk time while the others leave.

Long Beach is one of many rallies which use the Wild Goose Chase as a bridge to their city's unchurched teens. A Wild

Goose Chase operates like a colossal treasure hunt for a goose hidden somewhere in the city. Busloads of teens follow a trail of clues. At each location they search for the person holding the clue by yelling "Goosey, goosey, gander?" The right person yells back, "Where shall you wander?" and hands over the clue. The last clue leads to the hidden goose which the winning team brings back to the central meeting place. When all the buses are back, refreshments are served and a short evangelistic message is given on the theme, "Christ, the end of youth's search for meaning in life." Variations include a Hippo Hunt and an Elephant Chase. Enterprising YFC men rent or borrow the big animals from a circus, zoo, or animal farm.

Miami runs rallies on a yearly theme: "Happenings—'68"; "Youthquakes—'69"; "The American Youth Market" ('70). They rent Jackie Gleason's scenery and stage props at minimal cost. Tuesday instead of Saturday is the big night for ten to twelve summer specials for each of which YFC rents a facility and charges admission: bowling alley, swimming pool, speedway (for Bug Nite), the ballroom of the biggest hotel in town (for comedy nite), etc.

Although they got few headlines for it, Miami YFC played a key part in the Orange Bowl Decency Rally which made national TV, *Life* magazine, and thousands of newspapers. It was a teen affair all the way with YFC teens in on the original idea, the planning and the production. Miami director Ted Place was on the four-man adult executive committee (which played a background part) and was also offstage emcee.

Campus Life magazine featured one of the key teenagers involved, Julie James, on its cover and ran her story inside. "As I became more involved in the decency rally through Miami YFC," she wrote, "I was amazed and thankful that there were so many wonderful people ready and willing to help in such a great cause. It is an exciting experience to watch how the Lord moves. It has strengthened my convictions that Jesus is the neatest person ever to have walked this earth. It has shown me even more that God is living and strong, and that his love has no restrictions."

The New World Singers, a YFC traveling group, are well received across YFC-land. In Denver, for example, they recently

A pillow fight
in Crown Point, Indiana
brings nonchurched to
YFC activities.

Left:
The "mummy wrap" in which
the most beautiful creation wins.

"Zap" or "shock-it-to-me" chairs
at secular teen fairs
pit one teen against another.
First off the chair at the signal
zaps the other with a mild jolt
of electricity. The booth
is so popular at fairs
that producers often beg YFC
to come in and set one up.

Competition for
the greased watermelon
provides wild action
at the Southern Area YFC
Conference.

Below:
Elephant Race in San Diego
drew nearly 10,000 students
to an outdoor stadium
to see ostriches
and elephants race
in city-wide
school competition.

They're off! With girls pushing and guys steering, contestants in a VW Bug Race go for the finish line.

A VW converted into a pop singer won top prize in Muskegon's Bug Race decorations contest.

Left: YFC serves the "world's largest milkshake." (Banana splits and other giant concoctions too!)

Above: Sometimes the fun gets very messy . . . but most of it is edible and the kids "eat it up."

The newspaper whomp is a current contest activity, part of a fast-paced series of games. Hundreds of kids from a single school may attend such events, then stay for spiritual dialogue with the Campus Life leader.

Right:
"Old Rubber Face" Leonard Rodgers, now director in Beirut, Lebanon, does his hilarious act for the kids just before leaving for overseas assignment.

sang and gave testimonies to a double rally (6:00 and 8:00 P.M.). Denver's weekly YFC Saturday Nites involve a variety of programs geared to teen interests, with the spotlight on one high school each week. Chicagoland also spotlights a school in each of its bi-weekly rallies. Recently Thornridge High School had 192 students there, including the school band and cheerleading squad. Because it was a record for a spotlighted school, the kids got the pleasure of "frying" Director Jack Daniel on the chair. Then an evangelistic message brought fifteen of the Thornridge kids forward for spiritual counsel.

Kansas City YFC, which dates from 1943, has rallies most like the old-time Saturday evening events. Director Al Metsker, the senior of all YFC men in experience, confounds skeptics by pointing to a full house every Saturday night of the year. But while Kansas City rallies may be old-time, they are definitely not second-rate. Pre-rally parties are held at points around the metropolitan area at 5:30 P.M. to whip up enthusiasm and hustle kids for the actual rally which comes two hours later.

The kids (both black and white) and relatively few adults jam into the YFC auditorium at 7:30. Kansas City YFC owns its own auditorium and facilities, worth a million dollars. Gospel choruses, folk songs, and hymns are followed by skits, audience participation funnies, and an attendance contest with a door prize. Director Metsker previews coming rallies and a local pastor prays. Key high schoolers give testimonies and a young preacher delivers a hard-hitting sermon and challenges kids who want to know God in a personal way to come to the prayer room. At the strains of "Just As I Am" twenty or so come forward. Then the audience is invited downstairs to the Rainbow Room for an hour of food and fun while decision makers are counseled upstairs.

A pretty Raytown, Mo., high-school student was one of those who went downstairs one Saturday night in Kansas City. A group of teenagers had invited her. That summer a neighbor urged Barbara Ann Rice's mother to send her to YFC camp in Arkansas. For some reason on the trip to camp her thoughts ran to her own safety, to death, to wondering what would happen to her if she died. Quietly she pleaded with God to help her understand the meaning of life.

"We had a wonderful time at camp," she wrote later. "Everyone was extremely friendly, but they had something excitingly different about them too. We met innumerable friends but the most wonderful friend I found was the Lord Jesus Christ. As God's Word was explained to me that week, I found He was the answer to life. I discovered that all these years I had been so busy living for myself, putting myself first in everything, I had overlooked the One who could do things for me that I could not do for myself. The true secret of finding happiness was yielding to Jesus Christ, letting Him have His way in my life. He would guide me and give me a purpose to live and die for. Life was suddenly beautiful.

"I came home and told my parents about my new friend. Soon they, too, trusted Him as their personal Saviour."

Rallies in all areas have used drugs as a theme for a YFC Saturday Nite. San Diego called theirs "Grass and Acid," and it caught Dottie Royal, a San Diego teen, on a night when she was "still hung over from the day before." The way she tells it, "I wasn't feeling too well that night and I had to get up several times during the rally and go out. But my curiosity kept bringing me back. I wanted to hear what the speakers had to say about their own experience with LSD and marijuana.

"A kinda young guy was speaking, and he really rapped! He said, 'Some of you kids sitting out there are laughing at us, and you're telling Jesus to "kiss off." ' I just kind of slunk down in my seat, because that was just what I was doing! I was saying, 'Well, Jesus, that's fine for people who want to go to heaven, but I'll take hell, because all my friends will be there.'

"But somehow after listening to him some more, I thought, 'Wow! This guy really knows what he's talking about.' He had been where I was. He knew what it was like. He had tried the same route and found that it didn't do anything for him. Then he told us about Jesus Christ and how He had taken away all desire for the stuff and had cleaned him up. He said that if we would just trust Christ, He would do the same for us.

"But I just couldn't buy it! Jesus forgive me? He didn't know how raunchy I was. He probably thought that I was really good and didn't know that I had done that much wrong! Anyway, I sat and listened to the whole thing and when it was time to go forward, there was a little war going on inside me. For one thing, I was dressed different from most of the girls, and they would all stare at me if I went forward. So I was going no, and Jesus was going yes—but finally I went.

"Several of us were taken into another room where some people talked with us and showed us what the Bible said about Jesus Christ and how if we would trust him, he would forgive all our sins and make us just like new again. After we prayed, I just couldn't get over how happy I felt. I didn't need liquor or marijuana any more, and I didn't have to try to find myself. I knew where I was!

"After that, I started going to all the YFC rallies and heard about the Campus Life Clubs. I thought I would give that a try, too. I was really excited about Jesus. . . . When I went to Campus Life Club, it was really great. It was so much fun! I had thought before that they would just preach at me and tell me what a sinner I was. It was so different, because they gave a positive outlook and told how much Christ could do in kids' lives."

Clubs and rallies are the main ministries of YFC. Youth Guidance (the name was recently changed from Lifeline) comes next; however, of the 228 U.S. and Canadian YFC groups, only 22 have a year-round ministry to troubled teens and only 87 are involved in Youth Guidance summer camping ministries. In a few areas YFC does not do Youth Guidance work because of similar programs by other groups.

Youth Guidance work generally begins with referrals from juvenile authorities. Referred teens are given special counsel and companionship; then, if possible, they are integrated into regular YFC activities. Some California groups take teenagers on retreats, hikes, and boat trips. Detroit in particular has a strong camping ministry with a full-time year-round camp director, Tom Wirsing.

A new type of YFC extravaganza is called an image builder, held to make the teen and the adult community conscious of YFC. The image builder usually is presented near the beginning of the school year and may be a concert, a banquet, a giant rally featuring a well-known Christian entertainer or preacher, or something unique.

A San Diego image builder was a unique haunted house that became a conversation piece on campuses all over the area. The ingenious Ken Overstreet, YFC's answer to Walt Disney, and his staff rented an old ten-room house for a hundred dollars and spent another five hundred spooking up the rooms.

During one week three thousand teens paid a dollar each to visit the house. They entered through a maze and slid down into a room where a solemn, black-suited mortician stood over a casket with a mummy. In the next room they came upon a man moaning on an operating table with calf brains and kidneys piled on his stomach and a knife seemingly imbedded in his brains. The man's arm was tucked under his side and a naked shank bone hung over the table. A friendly twist on the bone brought an agonizing groan from the model.

In another room they faced a mannequin hanging upside down with shank bones protruding. A small pump pushed blood up into the dummy to give the appearance of constant bleeding. A monster next to the dummy chewed on a bone, and as the visitor passed, he appeared to gulp a red liquid which he let drip over the bone.

Then spectators took seats in front of an electric chair with a man on it yelling, "No, No! I don't want to die." Suddenly lightning flashed and seconds later the wired spectator chairs jolted the watchers into the next room.

Still another room imprisoned a fellow with papier-mâché spiders scattered over him and three live five-foot snakes (non-poisonous) crawling over him. Then, as the visitors walked through a closet, surgical tubing dropped around their necks and sent them screaming into a room of headless monsters.

The haunted house is only the latest image builder San Diego has staged. One year they had the "world's largest hayride"—1,220 kids on trailers pulled by diesel trucks. Another year they had the "world's most unusual racing show" in which boys rode elephants and camels and girls raced in sulkies pulled by ostriches.

YFC men in conservative areas have not rushed to copy everything done in southern California. Bill Dyck in Winnipeg says frankly, "We're backed by a lot of good Mennonite folks. They wouldn't approve of haunted houses and using hearses for transporting club and rally equipment. Anyway, our kids don't demand this yet."

Year-end holiday retreats have been big all over since Roy McKeown and other Californians started them back in the '50s. One recent California regional holiday retreat called "The Living End" was held for three days during Christmas vacation. Admission was charged and each Christian teen had to bring a non-Christian. Five hundred rode inner tubes down snowy mountainsides, joined in a musical talent show, knocked off energy in snowball fights, and laughed through a New Year's Eve party that bore more than a slight resemblance to Rod Serling's old Twilight Zone television series.

A mad scientist and a time machine were on hand for the party. At 8:00 P.M., New Year's Eve, the scientist banged the machine. "Oops, I slipped," he mumbled. "It's eight in the morning. You'll have to eat strawberry pancakes."

The kids had been promised a steak dinner, but they ate the pancakes in good humor. They played noisy group games until midnight, then watched John Wayne and Kirk Douglas in *The Sons of Katy Elder.*

They slept from 4:00 to 8:00 A.M., ate a steak breakfast, then watched the Rose Bowl on color television. An evangelistic message concluded the affair with the result that fifty teens made first-time Christian commitments.

Early last year Chicagoland YFC made a small but promising start on a teen center in the South Side black ghetto. Each Friday evening the chapel of the Glad Tidings Gospel Center becomes "The Black Light." The pulpit is moved. Game tables replace folding chairs. Vernon Mitchell, a black Trinity College student and part-time staff member, supervises. "We're trying to help young blacks," says Mitchell, "to see that Christianity is not exclusively the white man's religion."

Chicagoland YFC has had proven success with a one-Saturday-a-month charm school for girls. "We wanted all of our girls to experience all of the balanced life," the charm school director, Karen Hutchcraft, a Moody graduate, said. "We developed a year-long curriculum and invited professionals—a beautician, a hair stylist, a cosmetologist, and a gynecologist—to give their services. About seventy girls, one-third of them black, paid ten dollars each to enroll. They were measured and weighed and their general appearance noted. To graduate they had to show improvements—lose weight, improve posture, and so on. Two of the first graduates now model professionally and all of the graduates serve as big sisters to girls enrolled this year."

Chicagoland also made a significant breakthrough into the assemblies of public schools that have a high Negro enrollment. Before recent school disruptions by black protesters, these schools were "unavailable" to YFC-sponsored speakers. But after the racial troubles, black evangelist Tom Skinner was welcomed by administrations as a calming influence and by militant young blacks as a young minister with whom they could identify.

A high percentage of YFC groups use radio broadcasting as an arm of their ministry, but Milwaukee goes further than any other, actually owning an FM station.

It started when director Vic Eliason and an amateur engineer, Larry Trumblower, met with some others to pray about a radio outlet for YFC. A week later a stranger walked into the office and asked if they'd like radio time. After ten months, however, they were cut off because of a change in station programing. They prayed again and within a week a station owner offered to sell them eight hours a day, seven days a week.

That cost more than they had bargained for, but then the owner offered to *give* them eight hours a day, seven days a week, for two weeks, so they could show people what Christian radio was all about.

With that they went to work. Trumblower bought a mixer from his own savings. Vic bought some turntables and they borrowed tape recorders, but after a few months they knew they needed better equipment.

They prayed that the Lord would supply a console. A week later at a local TV station they found what they wanted in a storage room—along with two RCA turntables. After some discussion they walked out with several thousand dollars worth of equipment for $350.

But when they got home there was no diagram nor instructions of any kind. They didn't know the function of even one wire. However, electronics had been Vic's hobby since he was

Tedd Bryson,
Great Lakes Area Veep,
uses the popular
roving mike approach
in a typical rally.

twelve and several others had some experience. They spent hours tracing each wire, cleaned and polished the unit and put it to work for eight hours a day—and it's still going strong.

From the beginning, teens helped man the station. Two alumni are now in missionary radio overseas. Other teens give sportscasts and help produce programs that have brought "decision" responses from many listeners.

Expensive TV time is harder to come by. Portland, Wichita, and Miami have utilized public service time, but Portland and Wichita are off the air now. Miami's "Teen Scene" is still on after six years in a nine to nine-thirty Sunday morning slot donated by the local ABC outlet.

Winnipeg YFC got a free booth at the Pan American athletic games, and many cities have worked summer fairs. Suburban Washington, D.C., YFC toured Virginia county fairs one summer with a sixty-foot air-conditioned trailer. At times they used the drivers' reaction test or the pie-in-the-eye machine. Every hour on the hour they showed a Christian teen film. In one week more than twelve hundred people came to the booth.

A summer musical group from the Thumb area of Michigan invaded beaches and, after entertaining, "rapped" with the kids about world problems, life in general, and the life Christ offers.

Right:
On Wichita YFC's own regular TV program, these three teens are hashing over the questions of communicating with parents, getting "grounded," and how Christ relates to these areas of life.

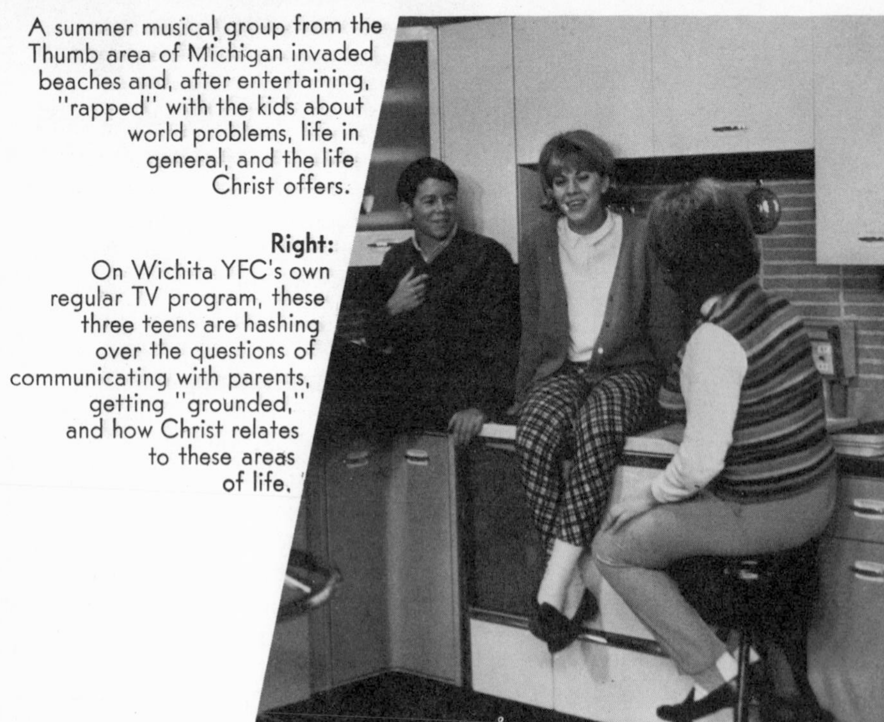

Chicagoland YFC had a "Balanced Life" booth in the World Teenage show at McCormick Place convention center. A big "Test Your Reaction Time" sign hit the eye of thousands of showgoers. Two Volkswagen bucket seats were mounted side by side on a three-foot-high platform. The test started when an operator pressed a hidden switch changing a signal from red to green. The first player to push his hand switch after the green light came on zapped the other player and sent him flying. If a player pushed his switch before the signal changed, he got the shock.

Some six thousand played the game and received a "re-volting" orange-colored card which read, "I got a charge at YFC." The thousands stopping by the booth were given the opportunity to take a balanced life quiz. Questions that probed gently into all four areas of teen life—physical, social, mental and spiritual—inquired into such things as whether the test-taker brushed his teeth and used deodorant every day or wanted to know more about God. In two shows more than four hundred teens made salvation decisions and were later followed up.

Such are some of the varied methods which YFC men use to reach youth for Christ. They may shock some tradition-bound adults accustomed to finding God only in the quiet sanctuary of a church. The hard truth is that these methods are reaching thousands for Christ who might never enter a church and probably wouldn't relate to what went on there if they did.

In Bakersfield High in California recently a senior student class leader, folk singer, and forensic star headed in a hurry for the lunch room one day. John Hanley was hungry. As usual, however, the long line of his similarly motivated classmates stretched out and separated him from the food tables.

John toyed with the normal ways of beating the problem—cut in on a buddy, get a friend in line to pick up a sandwich. Suddenly he remembered the "quick lunch" invitation a religious club offered every Thursday. Hurrying across the campus he smiled at the humor of the situation. There he was, the great atheist, hurrying to a YFC club because of a sandwich.

John picked up a bologna sandwich from the food tray, paid for it, then fought the urge to turn around and walk out. Honor forced him to take a back seat and sit through the program.

He also enjoyed it, tearing down the speaker's arguments—*great mental exercises,* he thought. *And a good lunch, too.* So he came back week after week.

About the fourth meeting John Hanley tore off the corner of his registration card. That was the prescribed way to indicate you wanted to talk personally with someone about Christ, and John was out for more fun and a good argument.

But the next afternoon in the club director's office, John Hanley's logic failed him. He heard the gospel again and, "For the first time in my life I had no argument," he said. That day in the Bakersfield YFC office John Hanley gave his heart and his life to Christ.

The change in his life was clear and the decision real, and it has reached into his home, his school activities, and his church. And it happened because a group of teenagers used a new means —a sandwich—to bring another teenager face to face with Jesus Christ.

8

Tale of Five Cities

Some 225 local groups, from one shining sea to the other, now pledge to North American YFC's doctrinal statement and charter. Some seek out the now generation in the troubled and much publicized cities. Others work with kids in the well-trimmed white suburbs. More work in small towns, resort towns, boom cities, depressed cities—as far southwest as San Diego and as far north as Edmonton, Alberta.

The main emphasis of all is evangelism which the following five profiles show. The philosophy and approach vary to fit the situation, but in one other way they are similar—all are winning thousands of teenagers to Jesus Christ.

CHICAGO (CITY)

Chicago is a city in a bind. Carl Sandburg might add a few lines today to his "Tool maker, Stacker of Wheat, Player with Railroads and the Nation's Freight Handler."

Many of Torrey Johnson's bobby soxers have long since fled the expanding black ghettos and are raising their own teens in the suburbs. Black students now outnumber the whites in Chicago schools, and the impatience of Chicago's one million Negro citizens has made a neutral or even passive position impossible.

One man who is not neutral is Jack Daniel, the slim, prematurely white-haired director of Chicagoland Youth for Christ.

Many teenagers and adults know Jack Daniel as the wisecracking, extra-quick-on-the-rebound funny man—the one they call on to give announcements at Winona because he keeps the house in stitches. They don't know the real Jack Daniel. His banter and sometimes stinging remarks keep many people at a distance, and few besides his family or those who work with him really know him. Still, teenagers instinctively know that the repartee thinly hides a heart which is easily touched and deeply concerned about them.

If Jack Daniel's first love is teenagers, his second is Chicago. Drive with him through the concrete tunnels of the Loop, north past the unique Marina Towers and through Old Town or along the lake front or south or west, which a third of the city's population—mostly black—call "home." Jack points it all out with pride. It's his city; he grew up there (in the super-rally days) and don't you knock it—even if he does.

Daniel can even sound a little like Mayor Daley as he talks about teenagers in Chicago. "We're going after a third of a million teens where they are and presenting the gospel which relates to them where they are. It's exciting.

"Our Chicago teens come in all sizes, colors, and interests," Jack explains. "Some are religious and others are as pagan as demon-worshipping savages in a missionary movie. Some of the former are in the blighted sections of the city and some of the latter are in the highly rated suburbs."

To reach about four thousand of these teens, Daniel and his staff direct clubs in forty-two high schools—some all black, some 99 percent white, and some mixed.

The thriving club at racially troubled Morgan Park High School recently included top athletes, three of the Ten Most Outstanding Seniors, and a Miss Teenage Chicago finalist.

The club was started in 1964 by two sisters, Renee and Roberta Toppen. They weren't sure the idea would go over at Morgan, but they recruited classmates from a number of denominations to give it a try. The first meeting drew twenty-five, four of whom committed their lives to Jesus Christ that night.

Morgan Park teens used the target teen concept and saw results. Jan Froemke took student leader Susan Hinchcliff as her target teen. Sue was in the Honor Society, French Club, Pep

Club, Student Council, Future Teachers of America and the Debate Club. Then at a YFC rally Sue faced God's concern for her and become a Christian.

In the following weeks Sue led her sister and her boyfriend to Christ and began bringing friends to YFC club. In less than a year, nearly twenty teenagers came to know Jesus Christ as Saviour through the persistent effort of Susan and her sister.

Steve Jemison, defensive back for Morgan Park's football team, and one of the city's top milers, was active in the YFC club until he graduated. Jemison happens to be a black teenager whose sensible, balanced racial attitudes don't always match his more militant brothers.

But the militant young blacks are responding, Jack claims. And one reason may be that Daniel understands their mood. "An increasing number of militant young Negroes possess a new awareness of color as something positive and distinctive," he says. "Not in the old sense that brought their ancestors shame, but in a way that makes them proud in saying, 'Black is beautiful.'

"If you are black today, you have to go somewhere, be in motion, be active in your thinking and attitudes. Then you state a position. Often, the more radical your stand, the more names you call your enemies, the better. But move away from any historic position. Unfortunately many leave the status quo far behind, even though they don't know where their new direction is taking them, and no matter who they hurt to get there."

The interest in blacks shows up in the Chicagoland office where wall photos portray attractive black and white teens having fun together. Some of the photos have appeared in *Campus Life* magazine, and Jack says he had "something to do" with getting blacks properly pictured and presented in the magazine. "I just told them we weren't going to sell the magazine anymore until it identified more with blacks."

Jack is also proud of the black men on his board, microbiologist Dr. Leroy Yates, a professor at Chicago Medical College, and Willie B. Jemison, superintendent of Buildings and Grounds at Moody Bible Institute. He wants more black board members and staff members to make the one black part-time staffer, Russ Knight, feel that he is not alone. "But where do you find them?"

he asks. "It's embarrassing to have an almost all-white staff in a city that has so many blacks."

Daniel also wants to move into Catholic schools. "We already have Catholic kids involved in every one of our public school clubs, leading, counseling, serving as officers. I know some say we should channel these kids into evangelical churches, but the way I look at it the kids aren't ours to send. Many, of course, do attend evangelical churches with their friends."

Jack reflects the restless spirit of Chicagoland YFC when he adds, "It's time for genuinely concerned adults to make sure that *all* of the high-school generation have an opportunity to find a meaningful relationship with the God who put Jesus Christ into history so that they may know what real life is."

CHICAGO (NORTH SUBURBS)

Drive northwest out of Chicago and you begin to realize why the pioneers called Illinois the Prairie State. The land is flat and the plain stretches for miles before gentle ridges break the monotony. Long before you come to those ridges, however, in what was once a rich forest of corn and wheat are suburbs with pleasant sounding names such as Elk Grove, Park Ridge and Arlington Heights. And the suburbs here have pleasant surroundings, good schools, and impressive church buildings. This is North Area YFC, and it coincides with the nation's top Congressional district, ranking first in education, income and employment. Teenagers in a town such as Barrington (average annual family income over $20,000) drive Thunderbirds, Chargers and Toronados to Campus Life clubs.

Clayton Baumann grew up in this area which he now directs for YFC. His father, owner of a music store in Arlington Heights, was an early board member for Chicagoland YFC. As a high-school senior Clayton helped start the first local club and after graduation from Wheaton College became the area's first full-time staff member at $50 a week.

Now, at 32, Clayton is the oldest of four full-time and six half-time staff members. He calls himself "the first among equals" and runs two clubs himself. "I earn the right to be heard just as my colleagues do."

North Area YFC gave up regular rallies three years ago. "We found that 99 percent of the crowd were Christians," Clayton claimed, "so we're now having three or four co-ops a year which involve at least half non-Christians—and no adults."

A co-op to North Area teens is an event for all clubs and may be a folk concert, a Campus Life Fair or a Spring Riot. At a recent fair teens paid to sling gobs of wet flour at a staffer perched on a chair. The Spring Riot offered water fights and a greased pig chase. Each co-op, after the fun and games, closes with an evangelistic message.

What about the club program? Does it effectively do the job of evangelism? To answer that two suburban North Area young men active in clubs in the last several years were interviewed.

Q.: John, what happened when you first started a Campus Life club?

John: We asked God to use our lives, invited our friends, and prayed. It was wonderful, yet the thing that concerned me was that we weren't winning kids. Well, we kept inviting, kept praying—and prayed harder.

Q.: How many were coming out in your junior year?

John: It started kind of small—five or ten kids—but sometimes we'd have sixty. I can remember one meeting when Bill Eakin came and we had a hundred and ten.

Q.: Who was president?

John: I guess I was. I can remember the first time we had unsaved kids come to a meeting. The first half-hour we fed the kids pies and the next half-hour we presented the gospel.

We would pray for these kids and we would give those in our club a chance to speak. We had outside speakers come and always there was prayer—prayer that God would save some of our friends. The first night the kids came, some accepted Christ. . . . We had the thrill of talking with them and introducing them to Christ. This continued.

Bruce: We got a big Southern guy that my brother and I used to hang around with interested in coming to club. He saw that Christians could have fun, too, so he started hanging around with us again.

YFC is involving bright high schoolers from all groups. **Above:** Four Chicago Campus Life leaders gather to talk about club activities in their high school.

Right: Steve Jemison, a young black Campus Life high school leader in Chicago witnesses to interested teens at Chicago's mammoth Teen Fair.

It's hard for us to fully realize that God answers our prayers—He hears and He cares about every part of our day, and He helped my brother and me. We really cared about Ed, and we worried about him. He was out stealing—bucket seats out of cars—but when the Billy Graham Crusade came along, Ed came to the crusade with us, and there God really spoke to his heart. He went forward, and I counseled with him. The Holy Spirit did something to Ed—He changed his life. Ed began to witness and it didn't take him three or four years like it took my brother and me. Now he's going to a Bible school.

When our senior year came around, the highest we'd hit before was 110 kids in our club. As we considered the 2,400 in school, we wondered what we were going to do about reaching more. So when we came back to school, we started our prayer meeting again the very first morning.

John: There were 55 kids who were jammed into the classroom. We divided up into six groups. They were desperately asking God, "Please use our lives. Please, God, give me guts enough to talk to kids in the hall."

They went out with this enthusiasm. I can remember in speech class kids standing up and saying, "The greatest thrill in my life was when I accepted Jesus Christ as my own personal Saviour." I can remember Bruce's brother standing up (his knees were beating a bass drum solo) and saying, "You know I have a pretty good police record with some of you kids in this room, but I want you to know that Christ has changed my life and it's different now." That was all he could say, but it meant a lot to the kids. And they started to look and they started to ask.

We finally got our club into the school, about this time. Yet at the first club meeting in school, only 55 kids showed up. We wondered, "What's the matter? Didn't anybody invite anybody else? We had this many at prayer meeting!"

Q.: How many came to the second?

John: We just about doubled our crowd. It wasn't until about the fourth meeting that we had about 150 to 160 kids. That was the first night God really broke through—11 kids really found Christ. It was a thrill!

Now we started to plan two or three weeks in advance. We had eleven teams and one kid invited 110 kids. The others weren't far behind him—they asked about 60 or 80 kids. About 400 showed up for one meeting.

Q.: Was there another meeting of this size?

John: Well, we learned to trust God and said, "Okay, Lord, what else can we do?" So we rented films and printed tickets and passed them out. We invited kids to the gymnasium one night and set up over 350 chairs—about 300 came. There was a poor invitation given, yet 10 or 11 kids went forward.

Q.: Bruce, you were on follow-up?

Bruce: Yes. When we talked with the kids, we gave them books and tracts. We encouraged them to pray and ask God to help them. These books really helped the kids get into the Word.

Q.: How many did you follow up your senior year?

Bruce: About 80 to 85.

Q.: How many went through the first follow-up book?

Bruce: Everybody did, and about three-fourths went through the entire series.

Q.: And most of them were followed up personally?

Bruce: Yes. You see, we were right there in school and the guys could get together with them and talk with them and that's what really helped.

This is one area where YFC gets overwhelming church support. Not only does 70 percent of the budget come from church pledges, but pastor after pastor in the area endorses the program —in spite of the fact that only one pastor sits on the board.

The pastor of a local Catholic church tells his congregation, "Send your teens to Campus Life clubs. They make good Christians out of them." A Lutheran remarked, "Our kids are getting good Christian experience, although some have little time left for church social activities—which isn't necessarily bad."

More important to Baumann and his staff are the comments that come from teenagers. "YFC has shown me that I shouldn't wait until I'm older to serve Christ," a senior girl said. "A girl friend for whom I had been praying for a year just accepted the Lord. I'm so thrilled I want to go out and tell everybody." And a former Catholic student claimed, "YFC has shown me that Christianity is relevant to gut issues like the race problem."

To keep in contact with their teens, North Area has a fleet of eight new Chevelles, bought at cost from a dealer. After office hours the staffers fan out to their various campuses.

"By 3:00 P.M. I'm on a campus waiting for kids to get out of school," says Gary DeClute. "I walk around, say 'hi' to those I recognize (back in the office I've gone over names and tried to visualize faces), talk to some teachers, and watch football or some other athletic practice. I may take one or two boys out for supper and a friendly talk. If it isn't a club night, I may tool around to school events and stop by a football game, a play, a homecoming dance.* I may not stay very long at any event. I just go to let the kids know I'm interested in what they're doing."

FRESNO

To hundreds of teenagers in Fresno, California, and to dozens of YFC men around the country, the director of Greater Fresno YFC is "Big Bufe."

Buford Karraker is a big man—240 pounds—brusque, and ready to speak his mind. To thousands who hear him as a dee-jay on Fresno's number one rock station he's a man who will listen to teenagers. To colleagues who know that the big frame holds a tender heart, he's a man not afraid to literally cry in his concern for teenagers.

Buford Karraker came to Fresno in 1954, right after school (Westmont College, Pasadena College, and Grace Seminary). YFC had been running in the San Joaquin Valley farming center since the late forties, but under Karraker the program has grown to include clubs in fourteen high schools, sixteen junior highs, a bi-monthly rally that draws nine hundred, and a staff of six full-timers, two part-timers and two dozen volunteers.

Fresno rallies alternate between what the staff calls the conventional and the non-conventional. The conventional includes music—secular and sacred—and a speaker. The unconventional is a Hippo Hunt, Wild Goose Chase or a Pillow Fight. It took twenty-five volunteers to clean up after their last pillow fight.

*Gary is one of very few YFC men known to stop at a high-school dance for PR with teens. A large segment of YFC's adult constituency puts dancing off limits.

Fresno's KYNO gives Bufe an hour each Sunday night from eleven to twelve for his "Teen Dialogue" show in which he alternates chatting with telephoning teens (no adult calls taken) and spinning pop records.

To discuss every conceivable subject from schoolwork to driving to dating to parents, teens call in with their opinions. The lines are constantly busy, and many complain they can never get through.

Though he picks topics carefully, Karraker makes no attempt to preach over the air or turn the topic to Christianity. But the clear indication from all opinions given on the show is that modern teens are aware of great needs in their lives and eager to find someone with some answers.

The subject is dropouts. A fellow calls to say that he dropped out of school because he was unhappy and wasn't accepted in any group because of his race and family background.

The subject is phonies. A young lady states that the worst phonies are religious phonies who hide behind a religious facade but live as they please. She accepts Karraker's challenge to look into the Word of God and find some answers. Next week, after the show, she calls to say that she did it, with her boyfriend, and that they both went to church.

Much of the payoff for "Teen Dialogue" comes after the show, when questions and problems come to light out of calls which come in. Listeners are invited to call after the show to talk to Bufe, to make appointments to see him, or to call his office.

Many times, on the Monday following the show and for days after, the Fresno YFC staff is busy dealing personally and by phone with kids with problems.

The problems vary. A girl called from a theater after seeing *A Hard Day's Night* for the fourth time. She was afraid to go home and face her mother.

A desperate young man called to say that his girl friend was pregnant, that he wasn't the father, but her folks thought he was.

Four weeks after the program began a young announcer and his wife met Christ in their own living room. A serious young man, he was almost out of place in the flash and ballyhoo which contribute to the big-rock sound. He had made a habit of staying around the studio when Bufe came in—just to listen, observe and ask questions.

He was well educated and thoughtful. But a boyhood in a broken home and his own unhappy marriage proved to him that he needed something more than he had available in himself. There were many late night sessions with Bufe, talking about God's claims on the life of a person, and ways in which faith in Christ can give one purpose and meaning for living.

Fresno carried out a pilot junior-high program for YFC, although Kansas City and several other spots have worked with junior highs for about ten years. The Fresno project, already programed by six other cities, is two-pronged. One part involves about twenty "image clubs" of four or five kids each with a college student leader. "We feel that the developing of junior highs needs an older guy or gal with whom kids can closely identify," Fresno men explain. The second part, "Teen Dimension," involves a meeting of all image clubs in group activity.

Fresno uses follow-up materials with every teen convert getting a series of six letter-lessons to be mailed back and graded. But, as with Chicagoland and North Area YFC, Catholic kids are not sent to Protestant churches, and Bufe has a part-time staffer who continues to attend his parents' Catholic Church.

Two years ago a Catholic priest friend invited Bufe to speak at a retreat for Catholic clergy. Later Bufe spoke at the priest's high school. "I put the balanced life chart on the board with Jesus Christ at the center," Bufe says. "My priest friend who really knows the Lord was blessed out of his mind."

Last year the priest came to the YFC fund-raising banquet. "A real conservative brother asked me," Bufe recalls, " 'Is he a Lutheran minister?' When I said, 'No, a Catholic priest,' he almost dropped his teeth."

TRAVERSE CITY

Flamboyant Bufe Karraker might have difficulty swinging YFC in the "cherry capital of the world," the town of 22,000 population in Michigan's northwest lower peninsula that boasts among its native citizens the state's present governor and one of

Togetherness
in a sundae.
Traverse City YFC
director Don Waddell
stands at left.

Several
YFC rallies
now operate
teen centers like
this one in
Traverse City,
Michigan.

the state's two U.S. senators. Traverse City is a tightly knit community of rugged individualists with $75 million in bank deposits, 1.6 million cherry trees in the surrounding countryside, a summer stock playhouse with Broadway talent, eleven city parks, four golf courses, seven ski lodges, a YMCA, a city youth center and forty-two churches.

Traverse City is also a conservative town with more than its share of over-75 citizens, a low, low crime rate, and a religious pluralism that will match almost any metropolis. The forty-two churches include Greek Orthodox, Mormon, Seventh-Day Adventist, Jehovah's Witnesses, and six different brands of Baptists.

The old-time one-shot rally went out of Traverse City before the current crop of teens were born. The new YFC, which is barely four years old, germinated in the minds of five laymen who "felt our kids needed something they could do together as Christians." Kenn Haven, local radio and TV personality, remembers that "most of the churches were too small to do anything for the kids and few had adequate youth programs."

Haven (who has three teenage children of his own) and four friends sponsored off-and-on recreational activities until they heard about the YFC program in Cadillac, fifty miles away. They invited Cadillac director, Ron Kendall, to start something in Traverse City. Ron began coming up a day a week to direct a new club program in the public senior high school. Interest grew and the five laymen organized a board with Haven as chairman.

Haven wrote to the YFC office in Wheaton for a list of potential directors. When he got no reply, he decided Traverse City was "too small for them to worry about" and went prospecting at the Winona Lake convention. This effort and other contacts turned up about ten prospects from whom Glenn Waddell was hired. The young Ohioan, who had been tutored by Bill Eakin, came to Traverse City from Akron.

Now after three years, husky Glenn (a former high-school football player) directs seven clubs, a monthly rally, and a rented Teen Center. "Our rally format doesn't follow the song-shout-sermon philosophy," he says. "We make it relaxed and friendly to attract kids who couldn't care less about religion. We use icebreakers, musical groups, and speakers who can get down where the kids live."

Traverse City's rallies usually average about two hundred, but a special event like last fall's "Scream in the Dark" for Halloween may draw three times that number. For this they spooked up an old barn, brought in a Christian folk singing group, and brought kids out in a motorcade with sirens blowing from a sheriff's escort.

Traverse City's juvenile crime rate is unusually low, but those who do need help get it. Five boys have been sent to one of Michigan's two Youth Guidance camps. On occasion Glenn rides with local police and once accompanied them on a narcotics raid. Once he served as defense counsel for a boy in court who had no one else to help him. For this type of help he has won the appreciation of the Traverse City police chief. "Glenn's doing a job with our youth that we want continued," the chief says.

Another warm supporter is Evert Carlson, principal of the rural Kingsley High School. "The Campus Life Club has helped our students have better attitudes toward elders and see more the value of an education," he comments. "We encourage participation with no fear of violating church and state."

Astonishingly, only a few local pastors have shown favorable interest in YFC. A Lutheran minister even told Glenn, "Get lost, my kids don't need you." Board Chairman Haven recalls a pastors' free breakfast to which the board invited twenty-six pastors whom they thought might be interested. Only two came. "After that we decided to stop pursuing the preachers." Havens thinks pastors are not enthusiastic because "they are primarily interested in their own groups."

One warm pastor supporter is Rev. John Losen of the East Bay Calvary Church who attributes his conversion to Lansing (Michigan) YFC. "We plan our youth activities to keep from competing with YFC," he says. "We preachers might as well face the fact that the churches can never reach all the youth."

Glenn believes pastoral interest is bound to pick up. He scrupulously avoids scheduling YFC activities on church nights and rounds up kids for monthly Sunday-after-church singspirations that rotate among churches.

"Things are changing," he says. "A few pastors criticized us when we first put pool tables in the teen center. Now they come in and play billiards on Monday mornings."

HOUSTON

If Traverse City is an example of a conservative American city, then Houston, Texas, is a shining example of the mating of American affluence and supertechnology. Houston has outgrown the image of the wheeling, dealing, big rich cattle and oil men. It works at culture, thrives as the nation's third largest port, and takes its role as space headquarters in easy stride. And while the city has generally shed the brag label, it has every reason to blow its own horn as the sixth largest and one of the most progressive American cities.

The story of YFC in Houston is a typical American success story, and the successful director is Dick Reinholtz, a soft-spoken, transplanted Milwaukeean who moves forward with all deliberate speed. Reinholtz has a Texas-born wife, two kids, a diesel-burning Mercedes Benz (to save gas) and his own home. "I could be happy spending the rest of my life down here," he says.

A YFC rally boomed in Houston during the late forties. The most famous convert was young John Robertson who drifted in from California, went forward in a rally, and confessed killing a liquor store clerk back in San Diego. Robertson went to prison, was paroled after a few years, stumped the country for YFC, then entered seminary.

Then, like an oil well suddenly gone dry, the rally folded. Dick came down in 1959 to attend Gulf Coast Bible College, and, remembering how YFC had influenced his life as a rebellious pastor's son, figured that was what Houston needed. So he wrote to Ted Engstrom. Houston eventually became the YFC Target City for 1959. Dick first worked part-time under an experienced director, Donn Kenyon, then took over in 1961.

The first years weren't easy. "I remember walking into a pastors' meeting," he recalls, "trying to smother my persecution complex with the prayer, 'Lord, help me prove that YFC is here to serve the churches.' After that I began trying to put myself into the shoes of the pastors, imagining how they feel about their young people."

Slowly a solid program took shape. About twenty Christian Student Union high school clubs started by Southern Baptists came under the YFC umbrella, and an equal number of new YFC clubs got under way. A small club at Smiley High School sky-rocketed to an average attendance of a thousand at a weekly 7:30 A.M. school rally. The club sparked a YFC "Teen Crusade" in the school stadium that reaped four hundred teen converts. Once-high juvenile delinquency in the area dropped out of sight. This crusade's success started a ground swell for a city-wide week of teen evangelism with two hundred cooperating churches receiving over seven hundred young converts.

Then came the Miss America debacle that almost sank Houston YFC in red ink. A promoter breezed into town to set up a rally in the Coliseum, featuring Vonda Kay Van Dyke. Dick and the trusting Houston YFC board gave him carte blanche approval to promote an advertising campaign. But the crowds didn't come as expected, and neither did the contributions. The day after the big rally, attended by 5,000, the promoter handed over $8,000 in bills, mostly for advertising, and left town.

Dick and the board met in emergency session. "We've been taken," he told them after explaining that Vonda Kay was innocently unaware of what had happened. "I hope you men will stay on the ship with me."

The board members stood behind Dick. They dug in their own pockets, begged money from friends, implored a few creditors (principally newspapers) to write off debts, and vowed "to keep future promotions under our local thumb." Then they moved ahead to build the strong program which YFC has today in Houston.

Dick supplies a pulpit most Sundays. "I preach the Word and don't promote YFC. That's the best promotion in the long run." He vetoes the appearance of local YFC teen musical groups in churches on Sundays. When he sees kids at a YFC event from a church that he knows is having a revival or other special services at the same time, he asks them to go to their church. When a Bible Baptist pastor told a girl to either give up YFC or her church, Dick told the girl to take the church.

Today Reinholz and staff reach some six thousand Houston high schoolers in fifty clubs and produce a monthly rally in the Music Hall that packs in up to three thousand at a time.

Ten of the fifty Houston clubs follow the new Impact/Insight format which Dick thinks is "the best thing ever to come out of YFC." The monthly rally in the Music Hall emphasizes "quality, variety, and content," and Dick auditions all musical groups. Last summer Dick and nine other adult sponsors accompanied seventy "Ambassadors for Christ," Houston teens, on a singing tour of Europe. Funds ($750 per teen) for the trip were raised in Houston. Dick's personnel goal is four full-time club

Houston YFC holds monthly rallies in the Music Hall, most prestigious auditorium in the Texas metropolis. "Good News" (marquee) is a Southern Baptist musical.

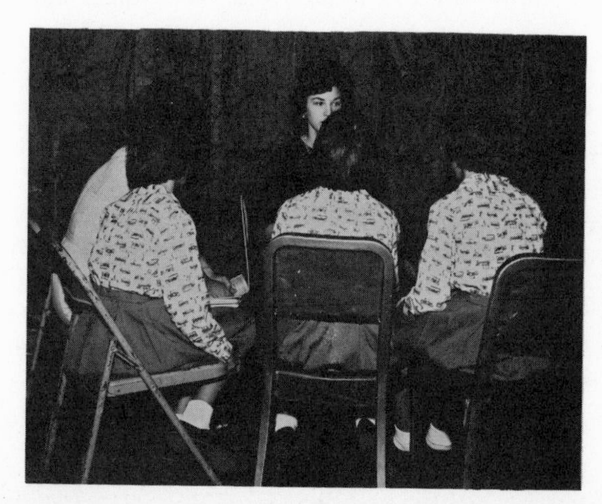

Houston YFC counselor Betty Pritchett talks with triplets who have responded to the invitation to accept Christ.

directors and enough volunteers "to cover every high school adequately." He sees his own future more in teaching and training; in 1969 he taught a course in youth ministries at Gulf Coast Bible College.

In the spring of 1970, Houston put major efforts into their "Happening." Paul Robbins, who worked with early Teen Teams and now heads YFCI's team division, helped Dick set up a three-week blitz on the city. The first week they contacted businessmen, high schoolers, clergy and parents, explaining goals and methods and getting the Happening completely underwritten.

Soon dozens of billboards, bus cards, newspaper ads and coverage promoted the big event. "The Young and Free" musical group (full time with YFCI) held thirty high school assemblies. Then, the second week, the Music Theater with 3,000 seats ran eight nights of Happenings, with a theme for each night: "The '70s—Age of Aquarius?"; "Please Don't Smoke the Grass and Eat the Daisies"; "Harper Valley PTA Revisited." Laughter, questions, music, and a thirty-minute Bible message by Jay Kesler on the night's theme penetrated the minds of thousands of non-churched young Texans. The third week, the Young and Free and some specially trained Houston teens followed up all who had responded to Kesler's youth-oriented speaking.

Dick thinks interest will increase in Houston YFC among Catholics and blacks. Priests now bring delegations of kids to the monthly rallies. Blacks recently ended a long boycott that stemmed from a walkout about ten years ago when an usher tried to segregate them at a rally. "A few are coming now," Dick says. "They know times have changed. We expect more."

9

The New Evangelists

The flight from Honolulu to San Francisco was the last leg of the trip home from the India Congress. It was January, 1959, and travel-weary delegates gathered in small groups in the early morning hours to recount the hectic days that had passed. After the Congress, teams had branched out for meetings all over the Far East. In Honolulu they had met again for the trip home.

Someone laughingly told the story of the group that went to Japan. In Osaka a swarm of Japanese newsmen and TV cameramen met the plane. Inside, the YFC men noticed the throng outside and wondered if a dignitary was on the plane. Then someone spotted a YFC banner and they knew the honors were for them.

The YFC men straightened ties as they moved toward the door, wordlessly arranging themselves in what they felt was their order of importance. The door opened and they marched out beaming, but the newsmen cried, "Where is the teenager? We want to see him!" At this, Steve Hope, a rally director's son and the only teenager aboard, moved toward the newsmen. The TV cameras ground away while the newsmen questioned young Steve on everything from world affairs to the Bible.

Many on the flight that night commented also that it was the Indian teenagers at the Congress who drew the teenage crowds and who impressed local pastors. It all added up to one thing in their minds—sending teams of teenagers abroad instead of preachers.

The very idea brought scorn from many quarters. "Send a group of kids overseas?" It couldn't be done. For one thing, what about school? And what could teenagers do that experienced missionaries and evangelists couldn't do better? Besides, there were too many risks in sending half a dozen immature young people into a foreign country. And if that wasn't enough to dampen the visionaries, the critics wondered out loud who would pay expenses. You couldn't expect teenagers to do that.

Ted Engstrom, Sam Wolgemuth and others back in Wheaton let the critics carp and handed the job of developing the first team to the versatile Wendy Collins.

In 1959 Wendell Collins was a slightly overweight, extremely popular youth leader who had already helped to pioneer several new YFC programs. As a teenager from Chicago's Southwest Side during the war, he had witnessed the grand beginnings of YFC. He had graduated from Moody Bible Institute, directed rallies in Wisconsin and Wyoming, and captained a gospel team to Scandinavia. But he was one of a new breed of youth workers whose know-how went far past the pulpit to probe the complexities of personal work with a troubled generation of teenagers.

In April, 1960, Collins headed for Europe, North Africa, and the Middle East to try the idea on missionaries and nationals. While some were doubtful, he received enough encouragement to set definite dates for a five-month tour the next year. In Beirut school principals found it hard to believe anyone could put together a team of teenagers who could produce a quality program. What's more, they reminded Collins, schools in Beirut were 50 percent Moslem so no preachers could go on the platform. Gleefully, Wendy accepted their invitations for a team.

In the States again, he carefully selected two girls and four fellows. All had above average musical talent and had been active in YFC. But Collins was looking for more than that. He wanted stable, mature teens—kids right out of high school who would willingly take a semester out of college and would trust the Lord for the thousand dollars or so it would cost them.

The team assembled on February 1, 1961, and Collins put them through an orientation program, plus hours of music practice. Three weeks later they left for Beirut. For four months the "Teen Team" (so called by an elderly lady in Beirut) stumped Lebanon, Greece, Italy and half a dozen more countries, singing, playing, and telling other teenagers about Jesus Christ. They held meetings in schools, churches, public halls, and street corners, aimed the gospel at 74,000 young people, and saw 750 come to Christ.

While in some countries—Lebanon, Italy, Switzerland—the welcome mat was out, in other places the reception was cold. After a fairly successful three months they weren't prepared for what they met in Germany. Berliners particularly made them feel unwelcome. The climax came one afternoon as they walked a West Berlin street. One of the girls was accidentally shoved to the pavement and came up with a bruised and bloodied knee. Another team member who came to her defense was struck in the stomach with an umbrella.

They returned discouraged to their rooms with talk of packing up and leaving for home—a month before their scheduled return. When Wendy came in he was at a loss for words but he made one request of them. "Let's pray, kids. But before you do I want you to sing for me the last verse of 'So Send I You.' " So they sang:

"So send I you, to hearts made hard by hatred, To eyes made blind because they will not see. To spend, though it be blood, to spend and spare not, So send I you to taste of Calvary." *

Then they prayed . . . and the tears came. On their knees they poured out their hearts and God spoke to them of the thousands of teenagers they had come to reach.

What really happened on that trip is best seen by returning to Beirut with Collins the next fall on a follow-up trip. After several days there he attended a rally for teenagers in the same hall where, six months before, they could find no teenagers who could sing together in groups. Now the entire program was run by teenagers. Before the rally ended, five different musical groups had taken part. The impetus, of course, had come from the Teen Team.

*From "So Send I You" by E. Margaret Clarkson. © 1954 by Singspiration, Inc. All rights reserved. Used by permission.

After the rally Collins asked to talk to the young people who were saved under the Teen Team's ministry. As they talked, many introduced someone else they had led to Christ.

Now there was no doubt about it. Collins went back and reported, "Many, many times teenagers looked at us and said, 'Why didn't someone tell us this before?' We'd respond that people have often come and preached this. 'Yes,' they answered, 'but *teenagers* have never told us this before.' "

With that report a new YFC program was born. In the nine years since, thirty-seven teams have been sent out to 70 countries. They've traveled more than 1,169,000 miles and held some 14,800 meetings with attendance of 2,900,000. Teen Teams have sung behind the Iron Curtain, on national television, in military bases, cultural clubs, opera schools, prisons, ice rinks, before presidents, dictators, royalty (including among others, Willy Brandt, Haile Selassie, Nehru, King Hussein, and Levi Eshkol), and one team took part in a wedding. Through it all an estimated 25,700 young people have come to know Jesus Christ as personal Saviour.

Collins was installed as the head of a Teen Team department that fall and began to develop an elaborate program. He printed detailed applications and sent check lists to local directors to rate applicants on scholarship, leadership, self-control, respect for authority, witnessing, appearance, initiative and other qualities. If the teenager passed this test, Wendy checked with his pastor. The applicant's parents came next, and only after Wendy received their consent was the teenager told he had been selected.

Hundreds of applications poured in. Local directors searched their city for the most talented teens. To have a representative on a Teen Team was suddenly one of the great honors in YFC. Collins scheduled two more teams for Central Europe and Scandinavia.

Collins was a natural promoter and he duplicated and distributed heart-touching excerpts from the letters those next teams sent home. From Holland, Gayle Moran, a sweet-voiced, trumpet-playing nineteen-year-old from Michigan wrote, "I never thought there would be so much prejudice against Americans. Some students just laugh during our assemblies. But," she added, "a Dutch student told me of his school's impression of

This '69-'70 Teen Team met with King Hussein and penetrated Afghanistan.

The music and message of these teens was so effective in Europe in '68-'69 that for the first time a Teen Team was regrouped and sent back.

us: hypocrites, showy and wanting to display America and its materialistic way of life. He asked me all kinds of questions, and I got a chance to tell him why I believed the Bible. . . . This boy, with tears in his eyes, promised to read the Book of John."

Collins set strict rules for the teams, one of which was they must write to parents every four days and to him every week. In another letter Gayle wrote to Wendy, "I'll never forget my birthday breakfast, served by my German hosts—raw bacon and warm goat's milk."

Jim Fortunato, on the same team, told of reaching forward to pick up his accordion one night in a meeting in Portugal. He accidentally clipped the head of the man in front of him—who turned out to be Portugal's leading surgeon and the president of Lisbon's Christian Business Men's Committee.

From Scandinavia Bill Spade reported that he played the piano so hard in a meeting in Sweden that the piano lid fell on his fingers.

The type of reports that Engstrom, Wolgemuth, and Collins especially wanted, and quietly waited for, began coming in. They were reports of doors which were never open to adults, now opening for teenagers—and often in strange ways. They confirmed the YFC leaders' convictions that the fastest way to the heart of a teenager was through the life of another teenager —anywhere in the world.

The Central Europe team wasn't sure that any meetings had been scheduled for them in Switzerland. Before they left, however, they had held thirty-two street meetings and eight night crusades.

Local Swiss teenagers were particularly insistent that team members speak to a school principal who opposed their visit. After he had talked with them, the principal consented to have them sing for his forty male boarding students at lunchtime. But he was still concerned about a religious group coming into the school, so he rented a downtown theater, paid all the expenses and brought his 500 students there for a morning program of gospel songs and testimonies.

With the success of the second and third teams the program got into gear, and YFC has exported four or five teams a year since then.

One reason, no doubt, Teen Teams went down so well overseas was the strict set of rules each teen agreed to and the intensive training dished out in Wheaton. A standard first session lecture included Collins' now famous goldfish bowl theory: "From this moment until you return home you will live in a goldfish bowl. First, people will continually watch you. When you eat, walk, sing, rest—wherever you go—you'll be the object of attention and curiosity. Only rarely will you escape. Besides that you'll be part of a team of six not of your choosing. You'll be with them in the bowl, day after day, week after week; they'll be your constant companions."

Team dress is almost always conservative, although skirt lengths might change from country to country. Girls on a recent team put their hems up for Switzerland, lowered them for France and raised them again for England—all to strike a balance between local teen styles and Christian taste.

Toughest rule—and hardest to understand for most teens—is the dating ban. For the five months overseas they can't date each other or nationals—in fact, they are to avoid all appearance of any special interest in a team member of the opposite sex. (No teen teamer has later married someone from his own team, although teamers from different groups have gone to the altar together.)

They are to especially avoid the tourist image—no cameras hanging from the neck as they get off the plane, no souvenir buying when nationals are present. They live in national homes, must eat *everything* placed before them, get up when their hosts get up, be consistent in devotions no matter what time of night they get to bed. They're reminded that in national homes they can't "make themselves at home" as they might naturally do in America. In most countries they travel in, a foreign guest in a home will be an extraordinary event for that family.

Teams are told about culture shock, warned of standard questions on race and Viet Nam which national teens will throw at them, prepped on local customs and history—and drilled for hours in music.

The greatest lesson for many teens in the entire team experience has been learning to trust the Lord for his share of the expenses. On acceptance a teenager receives nine pages of instructions entitled "Now That You Have Been Chosen for a Teen Team" and in capital letters, he reads, "A TEAM MEMBER WILL NOT BE ALLOWED TO LEAVE FOR HIS ASSIGNMENT IF HIS PORTION OF THE FUNDS TO BE RAISED HAVE NOT COME IN." "I wouldn't deny a teenager that experience," Wendy often told worried parents. "The faith he exercises in these days before he leaves will serve him well in the tough spots a month or two up ahead."

It was during the first team tour that Berlin YFC director Bill Yoder put Collins in touch with the superintendent of schools in the Western sector of the city. At a tea with school officials, the superintendent issued an invitation for a team to visit all thirty-seven high schools in his district.

A year later seven teenagers, all from the state of Washington, landed in West Berlin to accept that invitation. Max Robinson, one of the teens, described a typical day for the team in that city.

"The day usually began when my adopted German mother brought me to life at 6 A.M. I hurriedly stowed away a big German breakfast, grabbed my mid-morning snack, and ran down six flights of stairs to the street.

"Bill Yoder, the director of Berlin YFC, had already been blasting the horn of our little blue bus for a couple of minutes. I jumped in the rear door with lunch, trumpet, and raincoat, and fell onto the modified church pew which served as our seat. The trick was to hang on to the pew for forty minutes, eight miles, thirty corners, and one hundred bumps, while we picked up the other six team members, and to arrive in presentable shape for the high-school principal at eight o'clock.

"We began the assembly with a package of American folk songs, then Nancy told the audience about American school life. Next we sang several Negro spirituals, usually the best-liked part of our program.

"During the rest of the assembly, Steve Bibelheimer gave his testimony in German, the team sang a few German songs, and Roger Peugh challenged the kids with God's plan of salvation through Jesus Christ. We always finished an assembly with one or two lively gospel songs in English.

"The formal assembly over, we split into pairs to visit classrooms where we met the German teenagers face to face. Unfortunately, we had to leave too soon, but we left printed invitations for the students to attend our city-wide youth crusade.

"In the afternoon we held street meetings, visited adult leaders, saw a few sights, and talked with German teens. And we were on our own. By subway, elevated trolley, or bus, we visited various students' homes. In these afternoon sessions, we saw a large portion of our goal accomplished—introducing the living Christ to these young people.

"Evening found us in a church meeting and by the time each of us headed toward his apartment and climbed the usual six flights of stairs, we were ready to hit the sack."

This team was the first, but not the last, to visit behind the Iron Curtain—and also to get a real scare in the process. As two of the team returned to the West through Checkpoint Charlie one afternoon, they were pulled out of line, and one was led to a cell by a young soldier. Another uniformed official questioned him and demanded a complete recounting of how he had spent his time and money. He was released shortly, but not without a new appreciation for his American citizenship.

The teenagers they met behind the Wall not only tore their hearts with sympathy but taught them a lesson in living they long remembered. Max recalled the East German fellow who accompanied him to the checkpoint. As they neared the Wall, Max boldly asked him how badly he wanted to escape to the West and to freedom. The youth hesitated only a moment, then declared, "I wouldn't go, even if I had the chance."

Max was taken aback, but the explanation came forth. "God has an important job for me as a Christian in Communist Germany."

Probably more care went into the preparation of a team to Israel than any other. The invitation actually came from the Israeli Ministry of Education and the team were guests of the government.

In kibbutz after kibbutz they put on a program of Americana, gospel songs and personal testimonies—not preaching, but relating what Jesus Christ meant to them.

What moved many Israelis was their frank admission that much Jewish suffering had come under the name of Christianity.

Liberia's Teen Team. The blessing was reversed when nationals adopted an American idea and toured America in 1966 to present the gospel to U.S. teens. President Tubman of Liberia, a Christian himself, helped with their expenses.

The team tried to explain that "there are two kinds of Christians—those in name only and those who in their hearts believe in Jesus."

"I can't stand Christians overall," one boy told them, "but what you said tonight got to me."

An American Jew, with tears told them, "It's good to meet some real Christians. I lived in New York most of my life and never met very many, but I understand exactly what you meant tonight."

A middle-aged woman at a Tiberias hot springs resort said, "I am a very hard woman, and I have suffered much. I cannot remember the last time I cried, but this afternoon, at the close of your concert, I was weeping because of the expression of love from you young people." "I shall never forget, as long as I live," a team member wrote later, "that blue indelible A-15803 on that woman's arm—her concentration camp mark."

At a reception before they left, government officials and team members all confessed the apprehension they had shared as the tour began. But, said an Israeli spokesman, "There has to be a first time for everything, and after nearly two thousand years, we have come to the place of something like this. We do not want it to be the last. We want you to come back."

YFC leaders overseas quickly appreciated not only how a team could help their ministry, but also the "teen-to-teen" dynamic at the heart of the program. Soon they were training and sending out their own teams. South Africa sent a team to South America. England went to Sweden, Germany to Spain. Korean, Dutch and Indian teams ministered inside their own countries.

In the spring of 1966 Liberia sent the first overseas Teen Team to America. Four Monrovia high-school students, complete with native dress and tribal instruments and talking about their faith in Jesus Christ, wowed high school assembly audiences.

After displaying an "engagement ring"—a solid iron ankle bracelet to keep the girl from running away—they explained the social revisions that had accompanied Christianity. Using a grotesque wooden face for illustration they told American teens about pagan gods, then related the satisfaction they had in Jesus Christ. Finally they tapped out rhythms on the tom-tom and sang several Christian songs in Bandi, Gio, and English.

The effect was electric; standing ovations were the rule. Principals raved about the "best assembly we've had all year." Students surrounded the team after the bell, firing questions about African culture and their faith in Christ.

The Liberians also turned out to be an exceptional quiz team, and at Winona Lake beat four American teams in the international finals before dropping out. When they did, however, dozens of white quizzers rushed to their side to express sympathy in losing or congratulations on such a great effort. After they left, Bill Pannell commented that "thousands of American kids now have some completely new ideas about Africans."

The first twenty-five American teams restricted their ministry to singing, playing, and speaking in meetings and personal work among teenagers (if you call five or six meetings a day restrictive).

In September, 1966, Ron Wilson, YFC's overseas literature director, made a European survey trip with Bill Yoder, then European director. Teen Teams had covered the ground well in Europe and had proved their effectiveness. Ron also noted a healthy climate for literature distribution all over Europe. One evening in the home of a YFC worker in a Paris suburb, they searched for ways to break the distribution bottleneck which plagues so much literature work. The obvious answer they thought was a new type of team—a Teen Literature Team.

The first Teen Lit Team landed in Holland the next summer and began working the streets of Utrecht with a handful of Dutch young people. With a new Dutch YFC magazine, *Aktie,* they haunted shopping centers, train stations, coffee bars—any place they could find teenagers—and in the first week put over a thousand magazines into the hands of local teenagers.

The four Lit Team members didn't count the kilometers they walked that summer in Europe. Neither did they total the people who said no, the slices of bread they fattened on, the cups of coffee over which they talked to European teens. They camped in a cow pasture near Rotterdam and roughed it in a run-down chateau in France. In coffee bars, churches, tent meetings, on the street, in caravans, they sang and told what Jesus Christ meant to them. Then they dutifully picked up stacks of youth magazines and pushed into the crowd to sell them and talk some more.

It began as an experiment, but the concept was a success by the end of the first week—and their diaries and letters were crammed with experiences to prove it:

"The marketplace in Helsinki," Ed Huntley wrote, "is a fascinating kaleidoscope of sights and smells. I sold a magazine to a teenager there one morning and talked with him for awhile. The next day I saw a boy sitting by a fountain eating strawberries and went over to him. It was my friend from the day before. He was interested in what he had read, but the old language barrier limited our conversation. I invited him to the night meeting in the big tent, and as our team sang that evening I noticed him in the audience. So I went down and sat with him. When the invitation came, he started crying so I led him to the counseling tent, and he received Jesus Christ as his Saviour."

Several nights later Becky Faircloth took her turn selling magazines outside the tent after the meeting. "I was exhausted that night," she recalled later. "I didn't feel like talking to anyone. But I picked up some magazines, asked the Lord to help, and went up to two Finnish girls at the back of the tent. They had already seen the magazine and had a copy. We talked awhile and I invited them inside. Later that night one of the girls went to the counseling tent and made her decision to believe in Jesus Christ.

"The next day I met the other girl at an open air meeting. After talking for a few minutes, she opened her purse, took out a candy bar and gave it to me. 'It's good chocolate,' she said. But she wasn't ready yet to make the decision her friend had made. We walked to the edge of the park and she squeezed my hand, and in the best English she could manage wished me the best. Then she left."

The Lit Team kids quickly confessed that they never really developed a great taste for selling magazines that summer. Tired from pounding the streets for hours, discouraged by few sales, they often arrived at an evening coffee bar with little enthusiasm for conversation with strangers. It was at these times, however, they found themselves leaning more on the Lord and on those evenings something happened.

Perry Reynolds had had just such a day while working near

Rotterdam. Positive that the evening would be a drag, he asked a Dutch fellow in the YFC coffee bar what he thought of the program the team had put on.

"Before I knew it," Perry said later, "Peter and I were deep in conversation about God and life and such things. (I called this fellow I Peter, since he had a friend with him who was also named Peter.) Before they left the tent that night, they both knew they should believe in Jesus Christ, but they said it was too difficult. So I challenged them to go home, think about it and make that important decision before they went to bed.

"The next night as I came to the tent, I Peter came out and ran up to me. 'I've found it, Perry,' he said. I was thrilled. Both Peters had brought a friend, Bill, and we all went into the tent. Over a cup of coffee we shared the gospel again. Now II Peter and Bill wanted to believe in Jesus Christ, so we prayed and they did just that.

"The next night I Peter brought his brother John. We sat down to study the Bible, and John said, 'I don't know what you're talking about.' So we went through it all again, and John believed in Jesus Christ. The story doesn't end here. I Peter and II Peter, John and Bill brought more friends. At least two more fellows and two girls from that group received the Lord, and I've heard since that the group is growing."

All team members are encouraged to keep diaries, though few do, and few outsiders ever read the accounts that are kept. In one instance, however, the diary of an unusually observant, emotionally honest girl from Wheaton, Illinois, provided a fresh insight to what happens to a teenager on a team. Sherry Nill was on a team that toured the Far East. After a little persuasion she shared her diary with Wendy. It took a lot more persuading to get her to release it for publication, but an edited version finally came out under the title, "Confidentially, Sherry."

In Tokyo, one week out, Sherry jotted, "As I lay my head on the cushioned pillow and rest my back on this fluffy (?) mattress, my thoughts are on only one thing—how on earth can people sleep on these things?"

Two days later in Seoul, Korea, her humor turned to pathos as she wrote, "What an unbelievable day! The Lord has really spoken to me through what I've seen. We were welcomed at the airport with a huge banner, a band, corsages and flower bouquets, and so many beautiful smiles. Our first stop after going through customs was a World Vision hospital where we saw children who were nothing but skin and bones, suffering from malnutrition. We sang there for some of the children and staff, then took a ride through a poverty-stricken area with homes of paper-thin walls. Oh, how thankful I am for what the Lord has given me! We have what these people need—not so much financial help but peace and inner joy and the gift of salvation.

"The missionaries here have been so kind. They understand what we're going through but have no intention of spoiling us—for which I am glad! The only way to break me is through extremes and this surely is one of them. Up at 5:30 A.M. tomorrow so I had better hit the hay."

The team was still in Korea, one long month later, when Sherry wrote, "I am completely, thoroughly pooped, exhausted. Am I making myself clear? We had three high-school assemblies during the day. Billy Kim has arranged so that we always have a time after the program when we talk to some of the school kids and have them ask questions.

"Had lunch at the Air Force Base and then a little time of our own. I got letters from Mom and Dad and one from Suz. There were 1,500 at the rally tonight, packed in like sardines. Thirty decisions made. I really felt like singing—maybe because I have something to sing about!"

By December they were with American military on Okinawa. Sherry's account of a day there shows the pace and conditions teams generally work under.

"Good grief—what a day! We had seven meetings and only one of them was less than an hour. They really put us in some tight situations! This morning we all taped ten-minute interviews and surprisingly enough I didn't do half bad. I'm on the air tomorrow morning. Then we had a ninth-grade-only assembly. Had lunch in a real swanky officers' club, then went to Toby's school for two assemblies in a row. My voice is just shot.

"Right after those we had an hour of Bible club. In the assemblies Marilyn played this song that everyone plays with the wrong note at the end of the phrase. Anyway, after the meeting a girl came up to her and said, 'I thought you did okay, I mean it wasn't *that* bad.' I nearly died when I heard that. After those meetings we went home for supper.

"We were off at 6:00 P.M. again and had an hour and fifteen minutes with the roughest group we've ever come across. Some were talking; some sleeping; some walking in and out—but some were listening."

Endorsements from missionaries, nationals, government officials, parents, YFC directors and teenagers themselves have fattened several folders in the YFCI office. The one YFC leaders quote the most came from Billy Graham after he heard the Washington state team report on their Berlin tour.

"I am convinced," he told a gathering of Congressmen, senators and ambassadors in Washington, "that the greatest evangelists of our faith are teenagers. The world will listen to what the next generation has to say. When I see teenagers like Youth for Christ are sending out on their Teen Teams, I believe there is hope for our world, and there is hope for peace.

"Modern youth want the Christian message undiluted. They don't want you to beat around the bush. They want it straight from the shoulder. When they get it in this way from another teenager they will respond with tremendous enthusiasm."

10

YFC Around the World

Kenny Wong went on the platform that night in Calcutta only because he felt sorry for Hubert Mitchell. Mitchell had come in response to a wire for help from the Calcutta YFC committee. But in setting up a rally he could find no one in the conservative Anglican churches who would stand up and give a public testimony.

It was 1947 and Kenny was a 22-year-old Chinese bank clerk. The war had forced him out of Hong Kong, and he settled, with thousands of other refugees, in India's boisterous big port in the northeast.

"It's not right," Kenny's girl friend protested. "You're not a Christian. You can't go up there and say you are." In spite of the girl's pleas, Kenny wrote out a testimony—easy enough because he knew what they expected him to say—and Mitchell passed it.

But on the platform that night conviction caught him. He stammered, finally stopped and couldn't go on. The Holy Spirit stung his heart and, embarrassed and unhappy he left the platform.

For two weeks he nursed a bitter spirit, and he pulled away from the church, from YFC and from his girl friend. Finally he gave in, and God gave him the grace for the hardest step—to go back to the rally, confess the lie and tell how he had then yielded his heart to Jesus Christ.

Kenny Wong was not the first convert under YFC overseas. No one remembers that name. And no man-made camera could have recorded the myriad of scenes year by year—an evangelist in a tent on the Dutch dunes, two teenagers in a greasy milk bar in London, a Teen Team in the Peruvian jungle, a rally in a Tokyo high school—where thousands upon thousands of lives were changed. It's the story of YFC for twenty-five years around the world.

Torrey Johnson said it: "Youth for Christ is an instrument of God, formed of the Holy Spirit . . . to work toward the final, complete evangelization of the world." Eight years later Billy Graham noted that it was in the summer of 1946 when "something happened which radically changed the entire course of Youth for Christ International. By the grace of God and under His leadership we leaped the oceans, sped to the islands, spared no money or men to carry the gospel as far as we could into as many lands as possible."

Today, a generation after Youth for Christ became international, what's happening on the world scene?

In 1951 YFC promoters claimed to be working in seventy-six countries, meaning that an approved evangelist had held at least one meeting there. Today they report national organizations in thirty-eight countries and missionary work in sixteen more.

Many countries where YFC once flourished, and where barnstorming American evangelists once attracted huge crowds, now have no YFC influence except through pastors and laymen converted under early evangelists. Changing world attitudes account for some of this. The American exporter of ideas is *persona non grata* in many nations. But the work of teen evangelism has gone on for twenty-five years without a break.

A Greek general's daughter from a small town near Corinth attended a YFC meeting where evangelist Dick Reynolds was speaking. After the meeting she complained to him that she was reading the Bible but not getting much out of it. Reynolds spotted the problem. He read several verses to her, explained them, then asked her if she would like to receive Christ as her Saviour. Later she wrote to the magazine editor, "I'm very grateful to God that I was in that YFC meeting that day."

In some ways the work overseas has changed along with the work at home. The emphasis on teens reaching other teens is a standard part of most YFC programs around the world. Ron

Wilson, working with literature in South America, wrote, "Aurora Bustamente had never impressed me as a particularly aggressive Peruvian teenager. Then one night recently, our *Juventud* editor visited the Bustamente home and the girl asked for a few magazines to sell to her friends. Reynaldo offered her ten and she scoffed. She would sell more than that. But her mother laughed, 'You don't even have ten friends.'

"This was all the challenge she needed. She took fifteen magazines, sold them, came back for fifteen more and sold out again. The third time she took thirty copies and we're waiting now for a new sales report.

"After she had canvassed her friends, she took out after relatives and the like—sold four copies to a cab driver. On the street in her neighborhood she ran into Tomás, a teenager who had modeled for an illustration in the current issue of the magazine. She promptly turned his friends into customers, and the last we heard she was on the trail of the handsome young Tomás' female admirers—of which he had many."

The world congresses, which once were an annual affair, began to skip years, and finally faded out altogether. In January, 1968, however, the congress concept was revived for a week on the island of Jamaica. YFC workers and teens from more than a dozen countries held 313 meetings and spoke to 184 school groups.

The island was papered with Congress promotion. The Governor General attended several meetings, and told teenagers that "a personal relationship with Jesus Christ is the most important factor in a person's and a nation's life." A pastor standing at the front of the auditorium one night broke into tears as he watched teenagers respond to the invitation to "accept Christ as your Saviour." His daughter was in the middle of the group. Besides guiding youth all over the island to Jesus Christ as Saviour, the Congress marked the beginning of a regular YFC program. German director Werner Burklin, who had directed the Congress, stayed on for a year to build the work and left only when a full-time national director stepped in.

Under the new YFC international structure North American YFC holds only one vote on the 38-nation council. Sam Wolgemuth was elected president of the council, "not because he is an

American," Victor Manogarom from India says, "but because we believed he was the best man for the job."

North American YFC still provides the lion's share of money and manpower assistance: thirty-five U.S. and Canadian workers with financial support for sixteen nationals in other countries, plus five or six Teen Teams each year. All that North America does overseas is now coordinated by the new Council of YFCI in Geneva.

Any worldwide survey of YFC work would be outdated as soon as it could be put on paper. Men are on the move constantly. New programs begin and, unfortunately, some fade out. At the Jamaica council meeting in 1968 YFC arbitrarily cut up the world into eleven areas.

South America has a regular rally in Lima, Peru, and several Latins work full time on the continent. In Brazil, American missionary Paul Overholt has rallies in Belo Horizonte, clubs that use Insight/Impact materials, a nationally owned camp, parent seminars, and a youth leaders' institute for church workers.

North of the continent, Keith Rowe, a native Jamaican, directs work in the Caribbean Central America area. Last year they reported more than one hundred clubs and fifty regular rallies, including Rowe's own rally in Trinidad.

In West Africa Director Al Snyder supervises established work in Liberia and Ghana. South Africa, under Dennis House, has rallies and clubs and features "Keen Teen Crusades." Here teens spend a week studying the teen-to-teen approach each morning, go two-by-two in the afternoon to contact all youth in a town or suburb, then present an evening evangelistic service where an average of 80 percent of teens attending are "non-religious."

Australia has some of the biggest modern-day YFC crowds—up to 2,500—for special occasions in Melbourne's Town Hall. Though not nearly as strong per capita as New Zealand, Aussie youth have rallies (24) and clubs in major cities with quizzing and youth camps.

In Southeast Asia there are programs in Singapore, Penang and Malacca, Malaysia, and an attempt is being made to launch work in Indonesia. Central Asia (India, Pakistan, Ceylon, Burma, and Nepal), with one-fifth of the world population, has forty-nine full-time staff members pushing rallies, clubs, literature, evangelistic crusades, and open-air meetings. The informal monthly rally in Nepal (where making converts is forbidden by law) is held in a hotel lobby. Central Asian youth leadership training schools have graduated over two hundred new youth leaders into other ministries similar to YFC.

Far East YFC under Canadian Jim Wilson has clubs and rallies and recently held a summer conference similar to Winona with quizzing and talent contests. The Middle East area, centered in Beirut, is directed by an American missionary, Leonard Rodgers.

European YFC has recovered from a long limbo that followed the phasing out of the North American evangelistic teams. Work now goes on in England, North Ireland, Holland, Germany, France, Portugal, Denmark, Norway, Sweden, Irish Republic and Spain.

Now for a closer view of YFC, follow me on a tour to four overseas areas.

SINGAPORE

This tiny 20-square-mile nation-city, a former pirate's paradise, exerts an Asian influence far beyond that of its two million population. British and American missions have sensed the strategic importance of the island where four great civilizations —Malayan, Chinese, Indian, and European—converge. But for all their activity, Singapore Protestants and Catholics still number only about 40,000. Ninety-eight percent of the population remains Buddhist, Muslim or Hindu.

Traveling evangelist Joe Weatherly and Kenny Wong started YFC in Singapore twenty years ago. Then Liew Kee Kok took over. Kee Kok was a teenager in Singapore right after the war and cites what he calls an early case of the teen-to-teen method which brought him to Jesus Christ.

"Just before the Japanese took my country in 1942, my father and I fled to the jungles of Malaya. We watched as tens of thousands of our countrymen were trucked away to dig their own graves, then lined up to be toppled into them by chattering machine guns. Many of our women were molested, and during

YFC girls' class on witnessing in Singapore.

Club meeting under a tree in Singapore. Students are from an all-girls school.

Singapore teens enjoy fun outdoors.

Boys' trio at Singapore YFC rally in ultramodern new Singapore Conference Hall. The rally is the largest evangelical service in the city-nation.

the four years of Japanese occupation, I became very bitter. To stay alive in the jungle, my father and I ate monkey, python, fish from the streams, and roots and plants, like sweet potatoes and tapioca which we cultivated ourselves. We often missed meals, but somehow we managed to survive.

"Then the Americans dropped the atom bomb on Hiroshima in August, 1945, and Japan surrendered. We returned to Singapore, but I was such a mixed-up, embittered, rebellious teenager that often I wished to go back to the jungle again. But I had to return to school, and at this critical point in my life, a classmate named David Ton picked me out to be his friend. He often paid for my food at noon and invited me to come to his home. We got to know each other very well through sports, studies, and just sharing experiences with each other.

"One day I asked him, 'Why do you do all this for me? I do

not deserve it.' Then he explained that he did it because he was a Christian, and he wanted me to know something about it, too. I was tremendously impressed by this, and eventually gave my life to Christ because of this classmate's influence."

Present director Daniel Ee and three other full-time staff members work with fifteen hundred teens in English-language Bible clubs (English is a required subject in Singapore schools), hold rallies that attract a thousand (half are non-Christians) each month to the ultra-modern new Singapore Conference Hall.

Singapore YFC is the only organization on the island working with juvenile delinquents, except for Catholics who operate a small "boys town." In addition, YFC promotes a film and literature ministry, sponsors "Keen Teen" crusades (similar to South Africa), conducts a training school for club officers, and enrolls each convert in a follow-up Bible correspondence course.

"We go crazy at our rallies," says Daniel Ee. "We have a band that can make fantastic noises, but the music is always sacred. Some adults think we jazz up the hymns and distort them. But the young people love it. We stress that the rallies are not for old fogies."

An active Presbyterian elder, Ee describes the generation gap in Singapore as tremendous. "Youth are usually not given responsibilities in the churches here. We give youth a chance to prove themselves and serve, and we find they grow up to be adult leaders in their churches."

Singapore and Southeast Asian YFC share the rented first floor of an old school building near the waterfront, with offices separated by a hall. Liew Kee Kok has moved up to direct the Southeast Asia office. Kee Kok—the name used by his friends—is counted one of Asia's top evangelical leaders.

Failing financial support recently forced the YFC man in Penang, Malaysia, to resign. Kee Kok, who receives aid from YFC friends in the U.S., left his wife and baby in Singapore so that he might fill in at Penang until a larger budget can be raised. With this accomplished, he plans to start YFC work in Kuala Lumpur, the booming Malaysian capital, and stay until a director can be placed and supported. "I'm always pushing to work myself out of a job," he says. While working in Malaysia, he must sandwich in trips to Indonesia and other parts of Southeast Asia where national churchmen and missionaries are eager for YFC to begin.

Kee Kok views the future with reserved confidence. "We can raise up national youth leaders to start work all over Southeast Asia, but we cannot support them for the first years. If only American Christians could see that they could support four national YFC families, who will win future leaders for the churches, for what it costs to support one foreign missionary family."

INDIA

For twelve years North American YFC leaders recruited men and money for youth evangelism in India under the warning, "Doors are closing." But, today, twenty-three years after the first YFC evangelists landed in the world's second most populous country, national YFC Director Victor Manogarom says, "Opportunities are greater than ever." He refers to what Indian nationals can do in youth evangelism.

Thirty-eight of India YFC's forty-four staff members are nationals. The foreign six are three Commonwealth couples, specialists, working themselves out of jobs. India YFC staff directs ninety-eight youth clubs, seventeen city rallies, training schools for church youth leaders, youth congresses with quiz and talent contests, youth-geared literature, evangelistic crusades, and Teen Teams in seven languages! India's first domestic Teen Team recently reached over five thousand youth in Madras and Calcutta in two weekend crusades and saw over two hundred make first-time Christian commitments.

India YFC is strongest among dioceses of the South India Church, a union principally from Methodist congregations. Victor Manogarom interpreted for Billy Graham during the evangelist's 1956 crusades at Palamcotta where six thousand were converted. Bishop A. G. Jebarha of the South India Church asked YFC to follow-up the youth converts. From this work a youth rally was started that continues in Palamcotta with over a thousand attending. And Bible clubs were begun in all Church of South India high schools.

A Madras Methodist pastor who supported Billy Graham's

YFC club meeting at a girls' school in Madras, India.

meetings says, "I wouldn't undermine Dr. Graham's ministry, but YFC is more effective. The clubs get right into the schools. There can be no disharmony between YFC and the churches. We work in mutual harmony and confidence."

There are two types of clubs. The more conventional YFC clubs are for twelve- to fifteen-year-olds. The second, called "Tami" clubs, are for those over fifteen and into their twenties. Rallies involve all ages with both native and Western music.

Thus far the evangelistic thrust has been to uncommitted youth who are nominal second and third generation Christians by inheritance. Law forbids Hindu school students from attending club meetings without written permission from their parents. Some Hindu parents have hurriedly married off daughters who became Christians through YFC. Still, Director Manogarom wants to "move faster to reach non-Christian youth who are open to the gospel."

India's economic plight and the cost of living affect the ministry in several ways. Manogarom reminds Western Christians that ten national workers could be supported for the cost of one foreign missionary accustomed to Western living standards. Indian Christians know how to sacrifice also. A teenage girl sold a pint of blood for ten rupees (75 U.S. cents) to help pay bills for the 1968 Asian Youth Congress in Madras.

LEBANON

Driving south from Europe you must cross either the Dardanelles or the Bosporus to get to Turkey proper. From there, all the way around the coast to the Atlantic, you're in a virtual Muslim monopoly.

On the very eastern end of the arc lies the tiny (pop. 2.7 million) Republic of Lebanon, with its shaky Christian/Muslim balance, desperately trying to maintain an independent stance in the volatile politics of the Middle East.

Beirut, Lebanon's capital, sits on a promontory jutting into the Mediterranean. At her back climb the Lebanese mountains from which Solomon hauled cedars for the temple. Sidon is forty miles south and Byblos, the oldest uninhabited city in the world, the same distance north. In her marketplace oil-rich sheiks and foreign traders rub shoulders with Marionite Catholic priests and Arab merchants.

Lebanon is YFC's Middle East outpost, an area where evangelism, to understate the case, is extremely difficult. Traditionally Lebanon has been a calm and open bridge between east and west. As such it has attracted dozens of Christian missionaries who see the city and its institutions as doors to more inaccessible areas where Paul once evangelized. But most find that the present Christian church in the Middle East is so weak that "it offers no light or salt to the surrounding populations"—to quote one Christian scholar.

Leonard Rodgers, a YFC worker from Kansas, is called by one Lebanese pastor "the only invited missionary in our country."

When Wendy Collins visited Beirut in April, 1960, local Christian leaders were interested in the team idea but a little skeptical that it would lead to anything other than just one more outside organization setting up shop in Beirut. To relieve their minds, Collins promised them that wasn't the case.

The team came the next year, ran through scores of meetings in a month and left four hundred young converts for Beirut's churches to deal with. A team of inspired Arabic Christian youth visited Egypt and won two hundred more. Collins made a follow-up trip the next fall and the pastor's committee in Lebanon spoke to him about setting up YFC.

Leonard Rodgers (second from right) YFC's man in the Middle East, meets with his supervising committee of national pastors and lay readers in a Beirut garden.

Arab YFCers at a foodfest in Beirut.

Quizzing in Beirut.

Reluctantly Wendy recalled his promise to them of a year before. But if they really meant business, would they write a letter of invitation to the International office asking YFC to come in? The letter came a short time later.

This request brought Leonard and Pauline Rodgers. Leonard had been converted in a YFC rally in Kansas and after college graduation had served on Al Metsker's staff in Kansas City for four years. He and Pauline had been interested in going to Lebanon under a conventional missionary society when the call came from Wheaton. "That the Lebanese pastors had asked for help," Leonard recalls, "was a strong factor in our going this route."

Len and Pauline have now been in Beirut six years. They have taken two four-month furloughs and were evacuated for a few weeks during the 1967 Mideast war. From the rooftop above their fourth floor apartment they can see the shimmering sea upon which the Apostle Paul sailed on his fateful trip to Rome.

Len's work is planned and evaluated by a YFC committee, representative of the four major Lebanese evangelical groups: Baptist, Church of God, Congregational, and Presbyterian. "Evangelicals are only one per cent of Lebanon's population and must work together," he says. "Some of my more independent-minded YFC buddies back in the States would say I work at a snail's pace. But we are building on the Church which will endure long past the time when the world has forgotten the organization we call Youth for Christ. As YFC workers, we are here to serve the churches by evangelizing and training youth. We consider every young Christian in Lebanon a *youth for Christ.*"

Lebanese YFC as led by Len Rodgers and national Lucien Accad has no high-school Bible clubs. "Why should it?" Len says. "We have a ministry to entire student bodies."

They have access to twenty-five private schools * which have an enrollment of about four hundred each. They speak in chapels, help young people present Christian programs, and confer with teachers about mutual concerns. Because YFC is the only religious organization working with secondary students in

*There are no public schools in Lebanon, only private schools which are operated mainly by churches and business and professional groups.

Lebanon, they have an open field. "This doesn't mean," he says, "that we can go in and preach and give an invitation to accept Christ. But we do win students to Christ and help them find places in the churches of their choice."

Lebanon's largest Catholic faction, the Marionites, is caught up in spiritual renewal. They now welcome Len and Lucien into several of their schools.

Len directs about four rallies a year in the largest available auditorium which seats only seven hundred. Last year Lebanese youth held their first Wild Goose Chase. About 175 followed clues through downtown Beirut, yelling "goosey, goosey gander" at every clue stop. One stop was a theater where fifteen more youth left the ticket line and accompanied them for the rest of the chase. After finding the goose, they assembled for food and inspiration. Twenty-one made decisions for Christ before the evening was over.

Last year Lebanon YFC also sponsored an Easter breakfast for church youth groups—a first in the country—and at another time held a youth retreat in a Beirut hotel where forty discussed spiritual matters until 2:30 in the morning.

Len and Lucien share a suite of offices in downtown Beirut with the minister-director of the Presbyterian Synod of Lebanon and Syria. Here Lebanese young people publish the bi-weekly YFC *Teen Time* magazine. Len estimates that the magazine (printed in both English and Arabic, with six hundred paid subscriptions) is read by six thousand Arab youth.

The political climate in the tense Middle East has limited organized YFC work to Lebanon. Because he is an American, Leonard cannot now visit neighboring Syria, nor can he speak in several other Arab countries which he is allowed to visit. "Our outreach is through the Christian young people converted while attending school in Beirut," he says. "This year new Christians have returned to their homes in Saudi Arabia, Cyprus, Iraq, Iran, and several other countries."

HOLLAND

George Brucks, the square-jawed, 44-year-old director of YFC in Holland is not Dutch—but he could fool most people. When he came from Canada in 1952 he drove himself day and night to learn the language and preached his first sermon in three months. Then he found himself a Dutch wife. But whether God called Brucks to Holland because of his Dutch-type temperament or whether Dutch qualities have grown on him isn't clear. What is clear is that he is as determined, as sensitive, and as frank speaking as any Dutchman ever was. And it is that determination which God has used in the ministry of YFC.

The quality showed up in George at an early age. Tough times in a small town near Saskatoon, Saskatchewan, in the depression years drove him away from home at fourteen. "I don't want to be a burden any longer to you," he told his parents. "I'll go and find work." So he hitchhiked cross-country, rode freight trains, slept where he could find shelter, and worked the rugged life of a Canadian lumberjack. In the middle of it God found him, and at nineteen he determined that preaching the Word was his calling in life. At twenty-six, he arrived in Holland as a missionary.

George saw the ups and downs of YFC through the years as he worked in Holland, and when the committee approached him to direct the work in 1965, it was down. "Unless something happens mighty fast," they told him, "YFC will fold up."

"YFC had become an anachronism in Holland," Brucks recalls, "and old methods had worn thin. For instance, youth in Rotterdam would rent a hall for five hundred and have only forty show up for a rally. Also, Dutch pastors had come to view YFC as outside church life, even disruptive to the churches."

"We are grateful for the methods God used in the past," George Brucks says. "But now we are using methods that work in Holland today, and tomorrow we'll use new ones."

One summer recently a circus-type tent, house-size, rose in a field by the edge of the Rhine River in Arnhem. Bicycles and motorbikes crushed the grass, and a steady line of fellows and girls darted in and out. Only the strains of "Bonnie and Clyde" or a Bob Dylan protest song, plus a small sign with the words "Koffie Bar," gave local Dutchmen a hint of what went on inside.

The first night forty or fifty teenagers came around. Some stayed; others went in search of friends. Word spread and for two weeks the coffee bar in the tent by the side of the river was jammed with humanity under thirty.

Much the same happened that summer in Middleburg and Delft—twenty or thirty tables, pop art, candles, a coffee machine, a platform, some folk groups, and a hundred or more Dutch young people in deep conversation well into the night.

Sit for a minute by this table in the corner. A trio is wailing a Negro spiritual, but no one's listening. At this table Arie's doing most of the talking. He's a student from Rotterdam and he's

U.S. YFC Teen Team singing the gospel in a Dutch "kaffee bar."

Holland YFC's director George Brucks and Dutch assistant lead devotions for YFC evangelist campers.

talking to Kees van Kampen. With a Bible open before him he's asking, "Does life have any meaning? Or are we all caught up in a great big machine?"

"That's what I thought," Arie says, "at least when I thought about it. And I thought, 'What's the use of trying? You can't beat the machine. If there's a God I'll never know it.'

"Then something happened, and I found that God is personal. I *met* him."

A Dutchman, young or old, is a reasoning thinker who makes no snap decisions. And Kees van Kampen was not easily convinced. But he left the tent that night a troubled young man.

For two weeks while the tent was up, the YFC workers spent the mornings in Bible study, discussions of personal counseling, and evaluations of the previous night's program. After lunch they took to the streets with armloads of Christian youth magazines and coffee bar invitations. Then it was back for supper and the evening's work.

Some of the curious coffee drinkers those long summer evenings left their skepticism in the tent and went away with a new confidence. They had long ago crossed off Christianity as outdated and meaningless. This was different, however. In the lives of the Christian young people they met they sensed an assurance of what life was all about and where they were going.

There was another side to the coffee bar as well. Take what happened to Tinneke de Vries—blonde, slender, a sixth-form student at the Lyceum. She might be the girl on the Dutch travel poster—the one with the tulips in her hand and the wooden shoes on her feet.

This Tinneke had on sneakers, blue jeans and a beat-up sweat shirt. She had become a Christian two years ago, studied the Bible, lived the Christian life, wanted to share it. Trouble was she didn't. Not only was she reluctant to talk to people about her faith, she didn't even know where or how to begin.

The first night in the coffee bar was torture for Tinneke. When she faced three girls who came in to look around, Tinneke wanted out. But instead of running she prayed—silently—asking God for strength, and plunged into conversation.

"What do you think of the coffee bar?"

The first question got little response. But it was an opener, and in short time she directed the talk to love and life and God.

Tinneke found out she didn't have all the answers and she admitted it. But she could tell her own story—what changed her life, gave it purpose, made sense out of nonsense. And Jesus Christ, through her life, became a person and a Saviour to the three girls.

It was all a revelation to Tinneke, that with beat in the background and a coffee cup in her hand, God could use her to bring the reality of Jesus Christ into the life of another.

"We reached thousands of kids with coffee bar tents last summer," Brucks says, "plus many more in coffee bars in major cities through the winter."

Dutch YFC still presents occasional rallies or concerts like the one they did with British pop singer Cliff Richard. They have no school clubs similar to those in North America, but new converts are drawn into Bible study and fellowship with a group of local young people. In Holland, as in most countries other than America, a local YFC committee is not a board of pastors or laymen. It's a group of young people who carry out their own plans and projects. Holland now has a dozen of these in major cities, each one active locally as well as working with the national office.

Any such round-the-world flying carpet tour almost surely misses much of the heart and drama that goes on in youth evangelism. Budgets, programs, plans, personnel placement are only props on a living stage where young people are meeting Jesus Christ and involving themselves in the world's greatest confrontation.

Sam Wolgemuth painted a human picture of the scene in a *Campus Life* magazine article shortly after he became president.

The scene: Stockholm, Sweden. A group of teenagers meet at 10:00 P.M., pray, then go off in twos to the theaters and bars where young people congregate to invite them to a youth rally at eleven that evening.

Later the rally begins, and the auditorium is packed. After the meeting a young man comes up to Paul, the speaker for the evening. He stares at Paul then asks, "Do you love me?"

Paul is taken aback, but he smiles and says quickly, "Of course."

The young man isn't satisfied. He looks at Paul more intently and says, "I'm serious. I want to know. Do you really love me?"

"Yes," Paul replies, firmly. "That's why we had the rally tonight. But more important, Jesus Christ loves you and died on the cross to save you from your sin."

As the boy talks, Paul learns that he was driven out of a broken home. "For years I found shelter in warehouses and under bridges. This is the first time anything like this has happened in my life."

In many ways the direct opposite of the Swedish boy is a South African starlet—beautiful, successful, popular. Teenagers in the rally are stunned to see her walk in unannounced. But when an invitation to come forward is given and she walks to the front of the room, they are dumbfounded. She enters the counseling room; the rally is dismissed; but no one moves. Fifteen minutes later she appears and tells the waiting crowd that she has accepted Christ as her personal Saviour.

Switch now to the *Student Haus* in the University of West Berlin in the time before the Wall went up. Roy McKeown conducts a youth crusade. He notices a large number of young people gathered together—East Berliners, judging from their dress and evident nervousness.

McKeown, through Gottfried Lauth as interpreter, invites those who want to accept Jesus Christ into their lives to come forward. But there is no response that night, and finally a somewhat discouraged group of YFC leaders retreats to the prayer room. Now there is a rap at the door. Gottfried opens it and listens to an East German youth who explains that the other twenty-nine in the group are waiting outside, all wanting to accept Christ as Saviour. They wanted to do it at the close of the meeting but were sure that an East German government agent had followed them and they were afraid to come forward.

That evening the thankful YFC team led all thirty of those young people to Jesus Christ.

11

YFC—A Continuing Miracle?

There are now thirty million more Americans under twenty than in 1947. Since 1955 over a million teenagers have been added to the U.S. population each year. *Look* magazine reported in 1967, "The tape measure and the scales prove they are bigger. A stopwatch will show they are faster. Any parent can tell you they are smarter, or, at least savvier. The FBI can prove they are more lawless. Most churchmen will agree they are more skeptical."

This year some twenty-nine million teenagers will spend up to twenty billion dollars on products ranging from surfboards to false eyelashes. Teen boys will purchase 40 percent of all men's slacks, one-third of all men's sweaters. Fourteen-year-old girls will buy cosmetics their mothers couldn't have afforded even if they had been on the counters in 1944. Fellows and girls will jet at youth fares further in one year than their grandfathers traveled in their lifetimes.

Via TV they will watch graduate courses in seduction in full color in their own living room that could not have been seen in theaters twenty-five years ago. Unmarried girls will have twice as many illegitimate babies as those of twenty years ago.

In school they'll yell words and phrases across the lunchroom tables that their parents didn't understand until after marriage. Then almost half of the graduating class will go on to college—compared with one-fourth that went on twenty years ago.

Teenagers have been YFC's special target for more than

six high-school generations, during the most frightening, dizzying and changing period in all history. When YFC began, man hadn't even touched the moon with radar. When the movement was just a few years old, there were only twelve regular television stations in America and large-scale production of TV sets hadn't even begun. The Pill, the jet plane, the computer, LSD and anti-polio vaccine were all in the future.

Those twenty-five years of YFC's existence brought on a new look in leisure. By 1963 there were a hundred times as many residential swimming pools in the U.S. as in 1948 (at the time of this writing there were 300,000). Culture became big business. Theater and opera attendance nearly doubled in the years after the war. Anthropologist Margaret Mead put it simply: "The world of today's children is as different from ours as our world was from the savages of New Guinea."

A generation gap? Yes! The chasm, according to Miss Mead, between adults and youth has never been wider. She told the 1969 Convention of the American Association of School Administrators: "World War II was the watershed and everyone who has grown up since then is experiencing a world which those of us of prewar generations just can't fathom."

YFC's Jay Kesler, who at thirty-four is half the age of Margaret Mead, agrees that the gap is greater than it has ever been. He points to world politics, the family, and educational methodology.

"The world political scene has widened the gap. In their parents' day war was an event. Now war is a way of life. Most boys today are asking questions before they go to war that their dads asked on the way home. They want to know, 'Are we always right?' "

Kesler notes that "parents are almost universally obsessed with *having,* while the kids are obsessed with *being.* Unlike their parents who were children of the depression, the kids have never known what it is not to have and cannot understand why parents are so obsessed with things."

Kesler also recalls, "When I was in school the teacher would look at a test paper and say, 'Johnny, you are a smart boy. You put down exactly what I said.' Today's bright kid may argue with the teacher all semester, then hear him say, 'You're my best student because you ask the best questions.' This 'why' generation is being taught to question everything they hear. Kids know how to get to the center of issues and how to ask the core questions better than adults. To get by in school they must think, contemplate, penetrate, project."

Still Kesler believes "there has never been a generation of kids more open to first-century Christianity than this questioning generation. True, their minds have been denuded of heroes by the all-prying press. But the rugged Christ of the first century who says 'Follow me,' is more attractive to youth than He has ever been."

Chicagoland's Jack Daniel points to the war, as well, as a force shaping teen life and attitudes. "The vast majority of teenagers," he says, "are depressed at the prospect of spending years and possibly their life's blood devastating a little country in order to 'save it.'" But, Daniel claims, "there is an even more deadly cloud in the teenager's sky, a radioactive one. We don't often see that awesome cloud in pictures anymore, but the Bomb is still there. Ask any aware young person or listen to their songs. No previous generation has had to live with it, but adults want them to act as though it didn't exist."

Last year 24,187 * teens in the U.S. and Canada made first-time faith commitments to Christ because of the ministry of YFC. One of those teenagers was Dave Balough, from Chicago's Morgan Park High School. For over a year Dave was the target teen of a football buddy, Steve Jemison. In the locker room, Steve talked to Dave about his faith. On the field and in school Dave watched Steve, watched to see if he demonstrated the faith he talked about.

Apparently he did. One night Steve persuaded Dave to come to a rally to hear a Christian ballplayer, and that night Dave gave his heart to Jesus Christ. "I'm a Christian now," he says, "because someone cared. Now my greatest concern is that some of the kids close to me might come to know Christ as I did. Maybe I can be the 'someone' who cares in the life of someone else."

*The number of teens participating in North American YFC clubs and rallies in 1968 totaled 231,227.

Many—perhaps most—of these 24,187 teens would not have been won by a church. According to the reports of YFC field men, most are now active in a church.

For a quarter of a century YFC has loudly proclaimed that it exists only to serve the church. While many church leaders may not admit it, the history of the past twenty-five years shows that YFC has benefited the church. Hundreds of thousands of youth have been converted and influenced to dedicate their lives to service within church institutions. Astronaut Major Jack Lousma, for example, claims that he and his wife are youth leaders in their church today partly because of participation in YFC when they were teenagers in Ann Arbor, Michigan.

Largely because of YFC, the evangelical church in particular has become aware of the needs of youth and adopted methodology to stay abreast of the changing times. Gospel choruses and more recently gospel folk music, youth films, youth follow-up materials, Sunday evening youth meetings with youth in charge, youth departments in denominations, youth directors * for local churches, Bible quizzing, teen talent contests, youth rallies and revivals, and traveling youth teams are some of the church's adaptations from YFC.

But what about YFC's relationship to the church today?

The veteran Don Lonie has watched YFC from inside and out for half his fifty years. Not one to pull punches, Lonie says flatly, "YFC's big mistake in the beginning was that it didn't work closely with the church. Now it does."

There are strong evidences that the latter is true. Certainly the intention is present as expressed by Sam Wolgemuth: "We are an arm of the church for the specialized area of youth evangelism—nothing more, nothing less."

Two isolated experiments may be harbingers for stronger ties between YFC and the institutional church. Eight young men in San Diego now divide their time between YFC club work

*The recent National Sunday School Association's study of teens in evangelical churches showed that one out of five boys interested in a church-related vocation would like to be a youth director. Before YFC, this professional church office for all practical purposes did not exist. Cf. Gene A. Getz and Roy B. Zuck, *Christian Youth: An In-depth Study* (Chicago: Moody Press, 1968), p. 52.

The counseling room (here in an armory) is still one of the most used spots in YFC rallies. Here, Christians point out Scripture to searching teens.

Southern Area Veep Willie Foote addresses an adult seminar in teen dynamics. YFC offers such seminars in many cities to help church leaders understand and work with youth.

and service as youth directors of local churches. Their salaries are split between YFC and the churches. In Wheaton, Illinois, Insight club groups are meeting on Sunday evening in local churches.

But do the churches need help in youth evangelism?

If we are to believe the reports of shrinking numbers of ministerial students and missionary volunteers and the polls which show large numbers of young people believing the church has lost influence, then we must say that it does need help. One might ask further, why do so many youth leave the church once they are out from under the pressures of parents? A survey on one state university campus showed that over 85 percent of the students "planned" to leave their former church. Why are so many students marching for almost everything and everybody except for what so many churches think important? Why, for example, would young activists at the University of California in Berkeley raise a banner in a Billy Graham meeting proclaiming: "CHRISTIANITY—NO, JESUS—YES"?

The signs on every hand show that the churches are having trouble reaching and holding youth. Will the churches accept help?

"My church will," Jess Moody, pastor of the First Baptist Church, West Palm Beach, Florida, told a YFC seminar on church relations. "We can't do much on the high school campus. YFC can."

David Mains, pastor of the new Circle Evangelical Free Church in Chicago, thinks churches in general "need" but are "not ready yet" to adopt YFC's present methodology.

Mains "grew up" in YFC. His father directed the music for an early rally in Quincy, Illinois. David was a YFC director for several years and met his wife through YFC activities. And he hands YFC the major credit for shaping the concepts that led him to establish the church which some call a prototype of the future evangelical congregation.

"The 'norm' of evangelical churches," Mains says, "is to speak with authority and expect people to listen. But the younger generation has been trained to probe and ask questions instead of accepting what someone says. We at Circle feel a church should provoke questions, encourage discussion, and permit people to

Above:
YFC president Sam Wolgemuth (center) discusses plans with headquarters leaders (left to right) Paul Van Oss, Bruce Love, Bill Eakin, Jay Kesler, Wendy Collins.

Left:
Dr. Sam Wolgemuth at his desk.

Below:
President Sam, with wife Grace beside him, addresses delegates at the '68 Midwinter Convention in San Diego.

freely form their own opinions without verbal coercion."

Mains sees the YFC teen-to-teen philosophy of evangelism as "rising right out of the New Testament. Peers can best win peers."

"Right now YFC is vital," he continues, "and is helping a wide cross-section of youth see that Christianity can be exciting and revolutionary. The typical evangelical church mostly reaches only youth within the so-called evangelical subculture. But YFC is going for high school kids of all kinds—those from theologically liberal Protestant churches, Catholic churches, pagans with no church background, and even the young black militants. If that isn't the New Testament approach, I don't know what is."

What about YFC as an organization? Is it still following its old motto, "Geared to the times, but anchored to the Rock"?

Warren Wiersbe, who once edited the YFC magazine and is now a Baptist pastor, is one of a few alumni concerned about the present drift of YFC. "YFC is geared to the times," he says, "but the anchor is beginning to slip. I'm worried about the trends."

Wiersbe is "for" YFC, "loves" the men in it, and believes "YFC did more for me in four years than ten in the seminary." He has "three to four hundred teens" in his church and says, "YFC should help the churches do a better job."

However, Jay Kesler does not see "theology as an issue at all in YFC today." He says, "We are thoroughly and completely seated in conservative theology."

Wolgemuth himself simply points to the doctrinal statement and says, "It hasn't been changed in twenty-five years. Our men still pledge to it."

In looking to the future, at the twenty-fifth anniversary Mid-winter Convention in Chicago Wolgemuth called for "top priority to be given to the exploding megalopolitan centers, beginning with New York City. Our overall North American goal is a club on every high-school campus. The American high school is generally open to Teen Teams and countries around the world are crying for them. We're emphasizing training now as never before. We're committed to establish a training center where not only can full-time YFC men learn, but where laymen can absorb the latest technique in youth evangelism and grasp

Above: Publisher Jarrell McCracken of Word Books, current vice-president of YFC, welcomes 2,000 guests to the 25th anniversary banquet. At right are Dr. and Mrs. Torrey Johnson; at left, Dr. and Mrs. Sam Wolgemuth, Dr. Billy Graham, Governor Richard Ogilvie of Illinois and Mrs. Ogilvie, and the governor's press secretary. **Below:** Cliff Barrows "does his thing" at the banquet.

WESTERN UNION
TELEGRAM

CLASS OF SERVICE
This is a fast message unless its deferred character is indicated by the proper symbol.

W. P. MARSHALL
CHAIRMAN OF THE BOARD

R. W. McFALL
PRESIDENT

SYMBOLS
DL=Day Letter
NL=Night Letter
LT=International Letter Telegram

1969 JAN 23 AM 11 54

The filing time shown in the date line on domestic telegrams is LOCAL TIME at point of origin. Time of receipt is LOCAL TIME at point of destination

DEB133 PD100

P WA245 GV GOVT PDB=WUX WHE WHITE HOUSE WASHINGTON DC 23
1153A EST=
SAM WOLGEMUTH, PRESIDENT,
YOUTH FOR CHRIST INTERNATIONAL, DONT DWR, REPORT DLY=
WHEATON ILL=

I AM HAPPY TO SEND WARM GREETINGS TO THE MEMBERS AND FRIENDS OF YOUTH FOR CHRIST INTERNATIONAL ON THE OCCASION OF YOUR 25TH ANNIVERSARY.=

=THE SPIRITUAL GUIDANCE AND IMAGINATIVE LEADERSHIP YOU PROVIDE FOR AMERICAN YOUTH IS A SOURCE OF SUSTAINING STRENGTH TO ANYONE WHO LOVES THIS LAND. AND IT IS PARTICULARLY SATISYING FOR ITS PRESIDENT.=

=IT IS GOOD TO KNOW THAT MY DEAR FRIEND, DR. BILLY

WU1201 THE COMPANY WILL APPRECIATE SUGGESTIONS FROM ITS PATRONS CONCERNING ITS SERVICE

GRAHAM, WILL BE WITH YOU, FOR I CAN THINK OF NO ONE WHO HAS DONE MORE TO STIR THE SOCIAL CONSCIENCE AND MORAL RESPONSIBILITY OF OUR YOUNG PEOPLE.=

=PLEASE EXTEND MY BEST WISHES TO HIM AND TO ALL WHO ATTEND YOUR BANQUET=

RICHARD M NIXON=

WU1201 (R2-65) THE COMPANY WILL APPRECIATE SUGGESTIONS FROM ITS PATRONS CONCERNING ITS SERVICE

Telegram of congratulations from President Nixon read at the 25th anniversary banquet.

YFC presidents, present and past, with Billy Graham: (left to right) Bob Cook, Ted Engstrom, Torrery Johnson, Graham, "Kelly" Bihl, Sam Wolgemuth. (Richard Ball/COMPRO Inc. photo)

the dynamic that makes YFC work in their community.

"They say we're grown up now," Sam reminded his mid-winter convention delegates. "I trust we have and that we have learned some lessons. If we aren't careful we can lose sight of the end—our goal of evangelism worldwide. We can become stratified and there will be no change. We can become pragmatists with a holier-than-thou phariseeism which is devoid of compassion and involvement. We can become so professional and sophisticated that we neglect the timeless affirmation of the Bible.

"Under God we must now continue the YFC miracle by moving out into the great population centers. The blacks and other inner-city kids are saying, 'Prove that you love us by moving where we are.' Unless we respond to the crisis in our cities, today's and tomorrow's Christian kids will have no choice but to take to the streets to express their disenchantment with the Christian establishment. If we truly are an arm of Christ and His church, we need to reach that arm into the area of greatest need. If the church is a willing servant of Jesus, it will seek to change its ways in this changing world."

Several nights later two thousand guests gathered at Chicago's Conrad Hilton Hotel for YFC's twenty-fifth anniversary banquet. Most of the old hands were there, the four past-presidents included.

Torrey Johnson rose for his few words. Twenty-five years ago he and a group of young radical preachers determined, with the help of God and in spite of the establishment, to reach young people for Jesus Christ. The movement they started completely revolutionized youth evangelism.

"YFC began in a miracle of personnel, emotion, and confidence, and the power of the Word of God," he recalled, "and the miracle of those early days has continued throughout the years."

Bob Cook added what many wanted to hear: "YFC has never become what some people feared—old men for God." Ted Engstrom added a word, then Kelly Bihl.

Finally, YFC's first staff evangelist and the world's best-known preacher, stood up. Tall and tanned and with a few wrinkles edging his intense face, Billy Graham lauded YFC's contribution in "concept and men for the work I have today." His voice rising and falling in a cadence cultivated in hundreds of YFC rallies, he declared, "During the past twenty-five years we've had a moral . . . and technological revolution . . . and we're now living in a student revolution. . . . Youth are now saying, 'We want something more than to learn how to make a living'. . . . They are an untapped resource spiritually and they are ready to march with leadership. I believe that YFC is being used by God . . . in reaching these young people."

When Graham finished, the lights dimmed. A musical group directed by a former YFC musician sang, and the spotlight moved to a banner proclaiming YOUTH FOR CHRIST—THE CONTINUING MIRACLE.

POSTSCRIPT: A Look at YFC Personnel

YFC staff men have always been individualists, impossible to pigeonhole, except that they subscribe to a common statement of faith (see appendix) and are committed to youth evangelism. Beyond this, they are still, in Bob Cook's words, "nondescript, individualistic birds."

But while the "typical" YFC man does not exist, some conclusions can be drawn from dozens of personal interviews and answers to a seven-page questionnaire completed for this book by 70 YFC staffers.

The staff is male-dominated, mostly aged 20-35. Only six of 404 directory* personnel are women, and all of the women are club directors except Ernestine Leighton in Wilmington, Delaware, who is a girl's Lifeline director.

The staff is white, not by choice, but by circumstances and past dereliction of involvement with black youth. However, several promising young blacks are interested and the door is wide open.

Half of the YFC men direct local organizations, with most of the remainder serving as associate directors and club directors. There are eight area vice-presidents, twenty-eight regional directors, twenty-five Youth Guidance directors, seventeen men at headquarters (including President Sam and his vice-president division heads), and a smattering of camp directors, music directors, and office managers.

Field men draw support from local constituencies. Headquarters personnel are sustained by churches and friends who view them as "missionaries to youth." Half of all the field men are in six states in this ranking order: California, Michigan, Pennsylvania, Ohio, Illinois, and Indiana.

Four out of ten hold liberal arts degrees. One of eight has a graduate degree (seminary or master's). One of four has graduated from a

*Most of the directory personnel are "credentialed," requiring a minimum of four years study beyond high school or the equivalent in experience in youth evangelism, plus two years of satisfactory on-the-job work. Those not "credentialed" are studying part time to complete qualifications. About 600 others serve in part-time positions. Many of these are expected to apply later for "credentials."

Bible school or Bible college. Alumni from Bob Jones University, Wheaton College, Taylor University, Moody Bible Institute are liberally sprinkled among the group.

Nine out of ten were "influenced" (conversion, dedication of life, call to service, etc.) by YFC while in high school.

One of three is a Baptist. One of five is a member of the Christian and Missionary Alliance, astonishing because the C&MA is one of the smallest (80,000 U.S. members) U.S. denominations. The remainder are about equally divided between "holiness" denominations (Nazarene, Wesleyan Methodist, etc.), The Evangelical Free Church, The Free Methodist Church, and various independent "Bible" churches. Most identified themselves theologically as "evangelical," with minorities preferring "fundamentalist" or "neo-evangelical."

Billy Graham led the list in votes for "most admired" in the Christian world. Other "patron saints" receiving substantial votes were Warren Wiersbe (second to Graham), black evangelist Tom Skinner, Keith Miller, Carl Henry, and Elton Trueblood.

More than half viewed Dr. Martin Luther King as a "great American" or a "great Christian," with some adding that he was a "theological liberal." The rest divided between seeing the murdered civil rights leader as "sincere, but too militant" and "a promoter of Communist causes." Younger YFC staffers tended to admire Dr. King more than older men.

Talks with YFC staffers from coast to coast indicate that many are moving out on social issues. Dick Hatfield in Grand Rapids, Michigan, for example, is "zeroing in" on inner-city youth, both black and white, with a downtown teen center (bowling, billiards, basketball, tutoring for under-achievers, coffeehouse, etc.). "If we are going to preach the balanced life," the lean Kansan says, "we must include the social. We can't bury our heads in the sands."

Ron Berrico in Washington, Pennsylvania, confesses he never had an insight into the black person until hearing Bill Pannell (the black ex-YFC staffer) speak in a YFC training school. "I discovered that evangelicals have been the greatest offenders to blacks, mainly just by ignoring racial justice. We're proud to now have young blacks active in our program. One is president of his student council and thinking of a career with YFC."

YFC men are not foot-loose and fancy-free in their local communities. They serve local boards which are autonomous, have the responsibility for hiring personnel, raising money, determining salaries, and sometimes own teen centers or offices (four out of ten boards do).

Boards are usually composed of white evangelical laymen, average about fifteen in membership, and meet monthly. Regarding the scarcity of blacks on governing boards, many staffers explained "none in area." A Californian said, "We're looking for some." This situation moves Bill Pannell to contend that "YFC's constituency is still too conservative to meet the needs that exist among blacks."

Why so few pastors on boards? Some comments from the questionnaire: "They're too busy"; "custom not to have them"; "bad past experience"; "create too many problems"; "cause bad feelings among denominations—if you have one pastor, you must have them all, while laymen's denomination doesn't seem to bother people."

Talks with board members in several cities revealed a desire to have voting representation on the national level. Only credentialed staff men can now vote in a national convention. Dale Ferrier, himself a member of the national YFC board, and long-time YFC backer in Fort Wayne, Indiana, where he is a leading industrialist, recalls that "board members were voting delegates until about six years ago when the staff men voted us out. They claimed we were 'not sufficiently informed.' I don't agree." The YFCI board is now considering reinstating local board members' votes.

Slightly more than half of the YFC staffers in the survey said they met their budgets, with most of the money coming from individual pledges gathered up at the annual fund-raising banquet. Some funds come from church pledges, although a few local directors don't solicit from this source.

Almost all church gifts come from Protestant churches. Only two of the seventy YFC staffers said they got help from a Catholic church, but, undoubtedly, many YFC groups receive gifts from individual Catholics.

How do they meet budget deficits? Pancake days, car washes, and candy sales with teens furnishing the manpower help plug many dollar gaps. Golf tournaments have erased the red ink in several places. And one YFC local earned $1,000 in twelve hours with a "tree planting."

But what happens when special fund-raising doesn't fill the till? Among the cryptic answers by YFC staffers were: "I run," "we stew," "we pray a lot," "we pay bills and hold up salaries," and "we take out personal loans."

Apparently middle-of-the road evangelical churches, both independent and of various small denominations, back YFC the best—"the kind that back Billy Graham when he comes to town," says one veteran YFC man.

The YFC staff survey indicated that large denominational churches show the greatest "indifference" to YFC ministries. Why? "Too denominationally oriented" (cited about Southern Baptists); "think we're too conservative and emphasize the new birth too much (Methodists and Episcopalians)"; "afraid of losing teens" (said of many denominations).

"The ultras" was the way one YFC man described churches showing "greatest opposition." Why? "When you have a corner on the truth, everything else is false." "We're not doing it their way." "We're supposedly too liberal." "We cooperate with Billy Graham and show his films in commercial theaters."

However, several YFC men reported exceptions to these generalizations. Chuck Rigby, YFC director for New York City, cited good Southern Baptist, Presbyterian, and Episcopalian support. The rally is held in the Episcopal diocese's "Cathedral House." YFC in NYC recently channeled forty-seven teen converts to a Presbyterian church.

An Illinois director notes that "while the General Association of Regular Baptists have not endorsed us on the denominational level, we couldn't live in many places without the support of local GARB churches. They buy what we have to offer."

A Michigan YFC leader saw methodology as the hangup of many conservative churches with YFC. "We're together in theology," he says, "but because I'm not tied to a system or tradition, some pastors don't understand me. Many conservative pastors feel that defending their system goes hand in hand with defending their theology."

Still, most YFC men enjoy rapport with local pastors. Seven of ten meet regularly with pastors and the same number "frequently fill pulpits." Half have "some dialogue" with local Catholic priests or nuns. A few hold discussions with rabbis.

The YFC staffers involved in the written study were assured that headquarters would not see their answers. This undoubtedly helped provoke the candid (and sometimes sarcastic) replies to questions regarding relations between field men and executives.

Except at the twice-a-year conventions, there seems to be little face-to-face contact between the Wheaton "brain trust" and those at the grass roots. Only two men outside of the Midwest said they had visited the seat of their establishment during the past year. "Seldom," "never," and "once every five or ten years" were typical comments.

The area vice-presidents are supposed to keep the lines open between Wheaton and the field men. But the question, "How often does the area veep or a headquarters executive visit your community?" brought a variety of answers, some of which reveal squeaks in the machine.

Satisfied field men noted from two to six visits a year. Gripers' comments included, "Not since I got here," "only when I have them speak," "depends on how much money we offer them," "when there's trouble or a meeting," and "I understand they do come through the area but I've never seen any of them." Apparently no uniform system of field visitation has been followed by the YFC brass.

Three of four field men think "the national office listens well to my criticisms and suggestions." The less happy remarked, "sometimes," "listen but don't respond," and "the individual director is just a peon unless he is a wheel."

Slightly over half of the seventy are happy with the present program pushed from Wheaton. Only one of ten thought YFC has moved "too far" from the big rally days of Torrey Johnson's time. Over a third said YFC has not gone "far enough."

Only one in five wants to sit behind the North American president's desk. Many more presented "bright" ideas they would like to see acted upon.

—Demand more from credentialed men and at the same time do more for them.
—Decentralize.
—Tighten up and have more central control.
—Set up an office that would be sensitive to the feelings of the smallest director.
—Open up channels so that all men will know what's going on.
—Bring field men into the national office regularly to glean ideas.
—Outline a plan of promotion from the field to the national office.
—Provide a personnel placement and transfer policy.
—Establish a retirement plan.
—Force local boards to pay a minimum salary. (Presently, headquarters *suggests* that local boards pay salaries equal to what local public school teachers are earning.)

All this does not indicate a vast dissatisfaction within the ranks of YFC staff men. It does reveal, however, that YFC is no closer to heavenly harmony than other Christian groups staffed by flesh and blood people. Any one who has ever sat in a preachers' bull session and heard men of the cloth gripe about their "headquarters" understands this.

Three-fourths of the seventy survey respondents want to make YFC their lifetime career. Only one in twelve said, "definitely not," and one in eight was "undecided." Significantly, all but one in the 22-25 age group said they plan to stick permanently with YFC and the exception thinks he "might."

But half of those above 40 expect to continue with YFC the rest of their working lives. One noted sadly, "Beyond 50, YFC looks uncertain for me. I'd like to stay in, but I must have financial security for my family."

This and the high ranking of *Consumer's Guide* and *Changing Times* (guides on saving money) as favorite magazines point up the dilemma of the dedicated YFC staffers. Their success in continuing to win high schoolers to Jesus Christ is limited only by the willingness of the older generation to support them.

APPENDIX

YOUTH FOR CHRIST INTERNATIONAL STATEMENT OF FAITH

- We believe the Bible to be the inspired, the infallible authoritative Word of God.

- We believe that there is one God, eternally existent in three persons, Father, Son and Holy Spirit.

- We believe in the deity of our Lord Jesus Christ, in His virgin birth, in His sinless life, in His miracles, in His vicarious and atoning death through His shed blood, in His bodily resurrection, in His ascension to the right hand of the Father, and in His personal return to power and glory.

- We believe that for the salvation of lost and sinful men, regeneration by the Holy Spirit is absolutely essential.

- We believe in the present ministry of the Holy Spirit by whose indwelling the Christian is enabled to live a godly life.

- We believe in the resurrection of both the saved and the lost; they that are saved unto the resurrection of life and they that are lost unto the resurrection of damnation.

- We believe in the spiritual unity of believers in Christ.

STRUCTURE OF NORTH AMERICA YOUTH FOR CHRIST

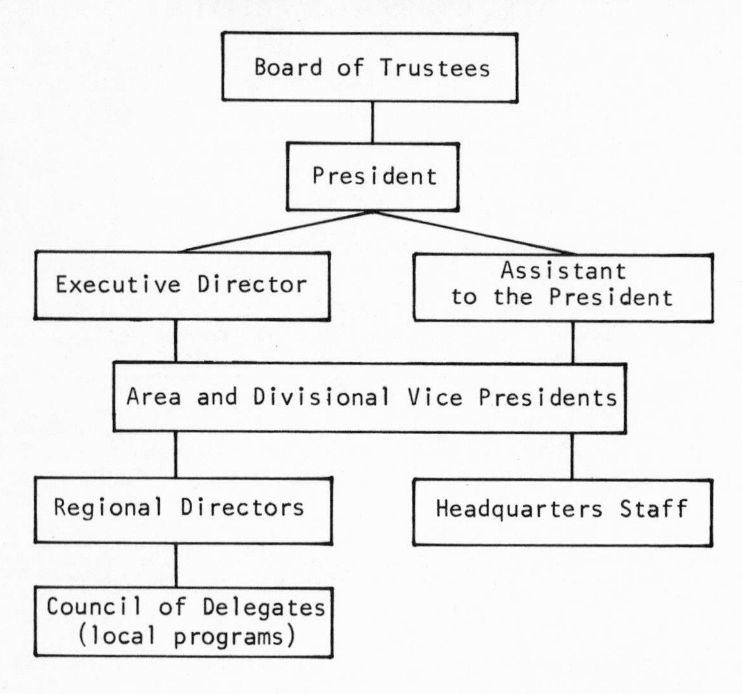

YFC AREA MAP

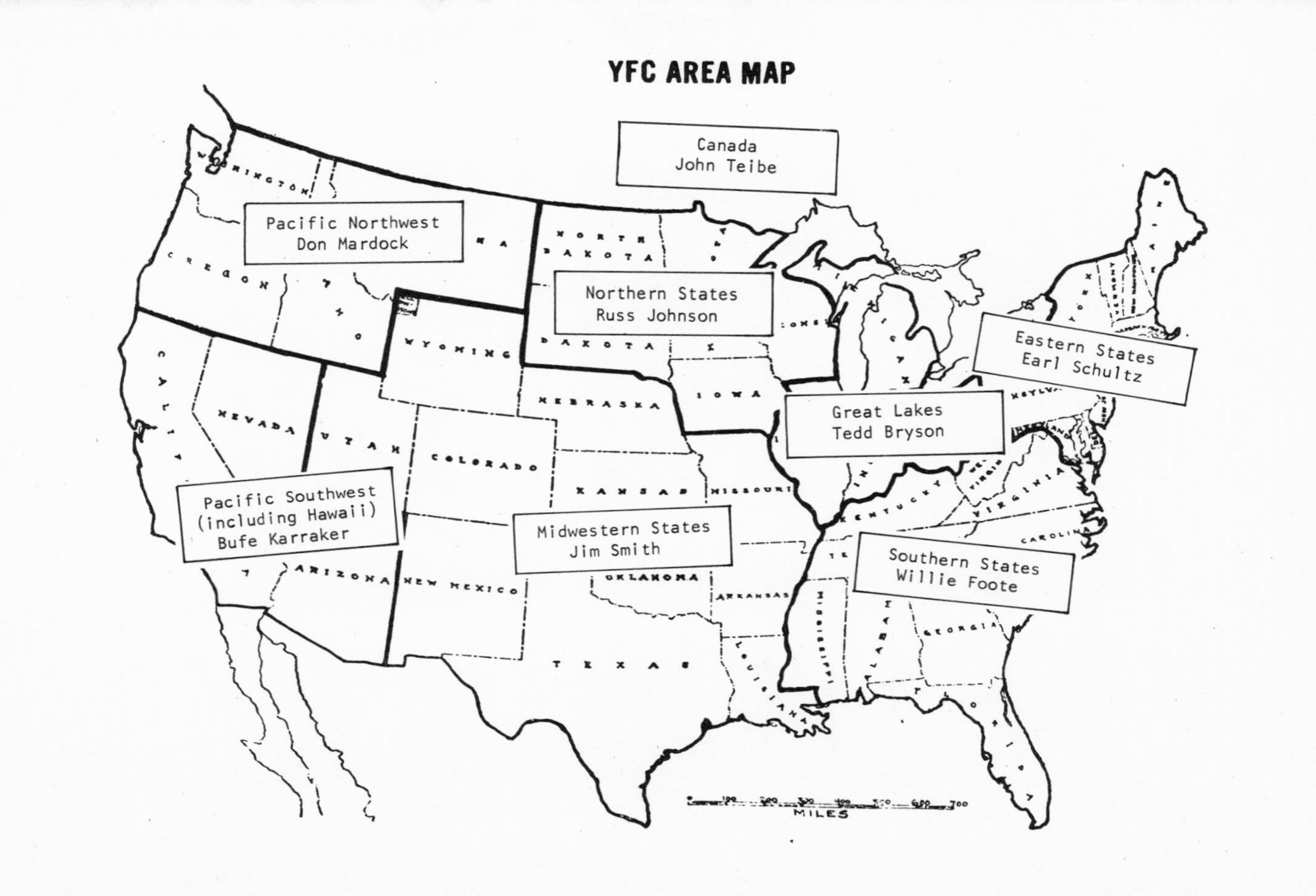

Canada
John Teibe
Pacific Northwest
Don Mardock
Northern States
Russ Johnson
Eastern States
Earl Schultz
Great Lakes
Tedd Bryson
Pacific Southwest
(including Hawaii)
Bufe Karraker
Midwestern States
Jim Smith
Southern States
Willie Foote
WASHINGTON
OREGON
CALIF
NEVADA
UTAH
ARIZONA
WYOMING
COLORADO
NEW MEXICO
NORTH DAKOTA
DAKOTA
NEBRASKA
KANSAS
OKLAHOMA
TEXAS
IOWA
MISSOURI
ARKANSAS
LOUISIANA
MISSISSIPPI
KENTUCKY
VIRGINIA
CAROLINA
GEORGIA
100 200 300 400 500 600 700
MILES

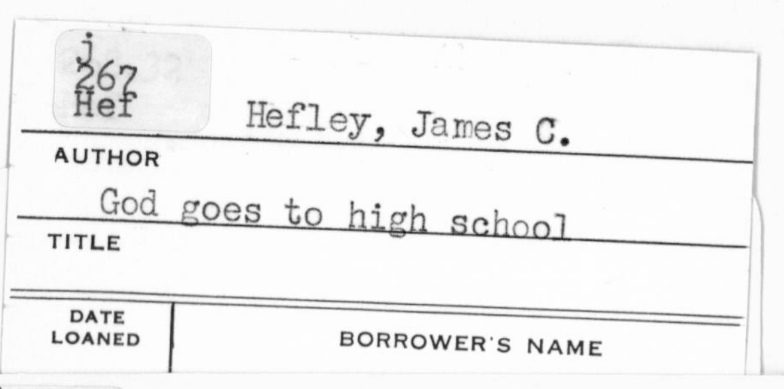